PROGRESS IN URBAN ECONOMICS

PROGRESS IN URBAN ECONOMICS

The Work of the Committee on Urban Economics
1959-1968
and the Development of the Field

by

Irving Hoch

Resources for the Future
1755 Massachusetts Avenue, N.W.
Washington, D.C. 20036

Resources for the Future, Inc.
1755 Massachusetts Avenue, N.W., Washington, D.C. 20036

Resources for the Future is a non-profit corporation for research and education in the development, conservation, and use of natural resources. It was established in 1952 with the co-operation of the Ford Foundation and its activities since then have been financed by grants from the Foundation. Part of the work of Resources for the Future is carried out by its resident staff, part supported by grants to universities and other non-profit organizations. Unless otherwise stated, interpretations and conclusions in RFF publications are those of the authors; the organization takes responsibility for the selection of significant subjects for study, the competence of the researchers, and their freedom of inquiry.

CONTENTS

List of Tables

APPENDIX TABLES

FOREWORD

This is the story of an unusual experiment. The experiment is still unfolding, but has reached a stage where stocktaking is in order.

It began some ten years ago when Resources for the Future (RFF) undertook to encourage research on the factors behind the use—and abuse—of the natural environment within the urban region. It quickly became apparent that this effort would be severely handicapped by the fact that very few economists were concerning themselves with urban matters. The quantity and quality of scholarly work in urban economics had not kept pace with the speed of urbanization in the United States, with its great impact on all facets of American life.

There were three choices. The topic itself might be abandoned; an urban-oriented research program might proceed, moving ahead within the existing quantitative and qualitative constraints; or a conscious effort might be launched to attract many more economists into the urban field, thus overcoming the existing constraints. Impressed by the severity of the urban problems and the fact that the very meaning of natural resources was changing under the impact of urbanization, RFF chose the third path. Here was an exciting challenge and the payoff, not only for the purposes RFF had in mind but for the nation as a whole, could be handsome indeed.

Discussions with Ford Foundation staff members revealed that they were equally concerned about the lag in the development of this critically important facet of economics. The Foundation made a special grant to RFF for the support of "an experimental program to advance the field of urban economics under the guidance of an interuniversity committee of scholars." To this end, the Committee on Urban Economics (CUE) was organized. Membership on the Committee included leading experts in the field from economics and other social sciences, with representation from a broad array of philosophies and types of universities. The invited members turned out to be a happy choice—dedicated, knowledgeable, and imaginative. They demonstrated a natural flair for "institution building."

The Committee set itself five objectives: (1) to encourage able scholars to do research in urban economics; (2) to strengthen university education in urban economics; (3) to seek out fruitful relationships of economics with other disciplines in developing a better understanding of our urban communities; (4) to improve career possibilities in urban economics; and (5) to improve communication between scholars and action groups, so that decisions, both public and private, within urban centers would rest on the best possible knowledge.

Looking back on the organization and a decade of operations of CUE, two innovative features stand out. The principal innovation of CUE was to get away from the traditional practice of parceling out support in an ad hoc fashion for miscellaneous studies by evolving a broad, long-range strategy for development of the field, ranging from fellowships and university support grants to communication aids. The complementary feature was organizational. Other interuniversity groups had been organized in the past to guide intellectual efforts. In this case, the unique feature was the substantive and organizational overview provided, during the first stage of the effort, by a non-university research institution; namely, RFF. A "lead organization" could assure both discipline and continuity in the many tasks undertaken. At the same time, a consensus by experts from different backgrounds and experience on what the field consisted of and which problems and activities merited high priority, assured that the limited funds available would be channeled into opportunities with high payoff potential.

Now, a decade after the launching of this effort in urban economics and after the expenditure of over a million and a quarter dollars, a recount of the history of CUE and an evaluation of its activities are in order. We were lucky to be able to recruit Irving Hoch for this task. Those of us at RFF who have been deeply involved in CUE from the beginning—Joseph L. Fisher, Lowdon Wingo, and myself—were too close to the effort to attempt an objective evaluation. Irving Hoch has been close enough to the CUE operations to be knowledgeable, distant enough to be personally detached. While members of CUE have provided many suggestions as to what should be included in a report on activities of the Committee, particularly on the questionnaire to the universities, the content and form of the report are Hoch's.

Hoch has done a remarkable job of tracking down the details of the CUE story, of summarizing the current state of the field of urban economics, and of flagging points at which the CUE effort may have been particularly helpful. He also highlights the fact that much remains to be done.

The latter deserves particular attention.

After a decade of "tender, loving care," urban economics is a fairly sturdy youngster. It could surely survive on its own. But, just as surely, it would grow more quickly and strongly if a certain amount of guidance and special assistance were continued. Given the limited success of the many hurriedly improvised action programs of recent years, it should be more evident than ever that there is need for sound social science research and for well-trained experts before our deep-rooted urban problems can effectively be addressed through action programs. Urban economists have a large contribution to make. Building on what has been learned and accomplished through

x

the experimental CUE effort, it should be possible to devise a "second-stage" mechanism and approach appropriate to the needs of the field and its just-evolving capabilities.

As of October 1968, some nine years after a Committee on Urban Economics was first established, Resources for the Future gave up its "secretariat" role and the chairmanship was turned over to Dick Netzer of New York University, who was charged with the responsibility of organizing a successor group. This successor group, an interuniversity committee, will have the task of overviewing the field and of guiding the various component efforts (on urban public economics, the conference on regional accounts, communication aids, and the like) into fruitful channels. It will also have to concern itself with the problem of ensuring that adequate funds are being directed into the field so that its full potentialities can be realized.

It only remains for me to express my deepest appreciation to the many persons who contributed to the CUE effort. Special thanks are due to Joseph L. Fisher, who, both as a member of the Committee and as president of Resources for the Future, provided continuing and effective support. Lowdon Wingo served as secretary of the Committee throughout much of its life and very little was initiated or carried through without his mark being on it. Wilbur Thompson and Irving Hoch served in the secretarial position for shorter periods, but also with distinction. My largest thanks are due, of course, to the non-RFF members of the Committee, and particularly those who served over many years. They served without any compensation, took on onerous tasks (e.g., on the fellowship committees), and attended meetings in every part of the country with unbelievable regularity. I can only hope that the fun of guiding a unique and seemingly successful effort was adequate compensation for the many burdens they have had to assume. I wish the members of the successor committee well.

Harvey S. Perloff
June 1969

Harvey S. Perloff, who was chairman of the Committee on Urban Economics and director of RFF's regional and urban studies, is now Dean of the School of Architecture and Urban Planning at the University of California, Los Angeles. Mr. Perloff is still associated with RFF as a consultant.

AUTHOR'S PREFACE

This is a personal, rather than an institutional report. It was undertaken while I was a visiting scholar at Resources for the Future, though by its completion I had joined the permanent staff. My assignment allowed me considerable latitude, including the opportunity to make rather broad-gauge evaluations. Some of the evaluations I made covered the work of the Committee on Urban Economics, which operated under RFF auspices. On the whole, I concluded that the Committee not only did a good job, but that it was an important job that needed doing. My institutional affiliation may lead to some question about my objectivity, or, as an RFF editor put it, of my attempt to play the role (as things turned out) of an "insider-outsider." Yet, on the basis of the evidence developed for this report, I concluded that I would be less than objective if I did not give credit where it seemed due. Under the circumstances, the reader may apply whatever adjustment factor seems appropriate.

Irving Hoch
Research Associate
Resources for the Future

PROGRESS IN URBAN ECONOMICS: OVERVIEW

INTRODUCTION

Urban economics is a burgeoning field. Its development has been received with growing awareness and interest. Yet, because the field is new, there are large gaps in knowledge even for those deeply involved and committed to the study of urban problems.

It seems clear that pressing policy questions in the area eventually would have stimulated the development of the field of urban economics. (Supply response to increased demand does occur in departments of economics). Yet it also seems clear that the Committee on Urban Economics (CUE) significantly increased the tempo, scope, and depth of the development of the field.

These introductory remarks are a springboard to the main purposes of this report: to review the state of the field of urban economics and to describe CUE's role in the development of the field. A third purpose, more tentative and more difficult to implement, yet probably of substantial interest, is to assess the work of the Committee as an experiment in academic innovation that may have applicability in the development of other subject matter areas.

Any field of study may be viewed in terms of its intellectual content or in terms of the institutional structure organized to develop, disseminate, and apply that content. These aspects are intertwined. The development of a viable institutional framework must reflect a coherent body of knowledge seen as applicable to important problems. The development of intellectual content in turn depends on its institutional base. A substantial number of specialists can work in a field only when the field has been recognized and jobs have been created and defined. The amount of work that can be accomplished depends both on financial support for the specialists and supporting activities and on recognition of the field by the more general professional community.

Ultimately, the growth of a field depends on the intellectual returns obtained from investment in it. However, in a dynamic context, the investment activity itself becomes a learning process and the pace and scope of development reflect the capacity to innovate, to experiment, and to respond creatively to experimental results.

In the case of urban economics, the history of the field can be represented in the following developmental sequence. There are a number of pressing,

1

practical urban problems for which policies must be developed and decisions made. These problems usually involve many people and much money. Thus, there is widespread concern with urban traffic congestion; smog; ghettos, blight, and riots; conflict of interest between suburb and central city; and sprawl, urban design, and the quality of urban life. In the past, a few economists worked on some of these problems on an ad hoc basis; others worked in well-defined fields touching on some of the problems. Some public finance economists were interested in metropolitan finance; some real estate economists, in general patterns of urban space use; and some transportation economists, in urban highways. After World War II, a keen general awareness of the growth of cities and attendant economic problems began to develop. And then a creative synthesis occurred, with the formulation of the idea that these problems and efforts could be organized into an interrelated field of activity. This made sense in terms of the application of economists' special capabilities. On a general level, the city itself is an economic entity—a social institution for economizing. In terms of particulars, the problem areas had important economic features that could best be analyzed by professional economists. (Other important attributes outside the domain of economics meant that economists would have to reach out to other disciplines as well.) The synthesis worked, the field took hold, and in the last ten years there has been an iterative and interacting development of institutional base and intellectual content.

This did not occur as a matter of course. (History does not feel deterministic as it is being made.) A number of individuals and organizations devoted considerable effort to the development. One of those organizations was the Committee on Urban Economics of Resources for the Future (RFF). The Committee, chaired by Harvey Perloff, was funded by the Ford Foundation through a special grant to RFF and in turn recommended grants to be made by RFF to promote activity in urban economics. It concentrated on the promotion of university activity, with particular emphasis on making urban economics available in Ph.D. programs. This made sense in terms of developing the productive plant (or intellectual capital) which in turn would produce a group of professionals with a high degree of competence. Further, this kind of institutionalization would, in itself, lend credibility and prestige to the newly emerging field.

The development of the Committee on Urban Economics (CUE) took place in two stages, each of which lasted approximately five years. The first, during which grants were made primarily to support the work of individuals, was exploratory. During the second, the Committee was concerned with building the institutional base of the field and concentrated on supporting programs in urban economics in universities.

The Committee recognized the need for incentives in high-risk enterprises. The uncertainties of a newly emergent field, compounding the inherent risks of doctoral candidacy, discourage doctoral candidates from choosing such

2

a field for their theses. By establishing a fellowship program and supporting the research of potential faculty advisers, CUE reduced these risks. Later, by means of matching grants, CUE helped a number of universities set up continuing programs in urban economics, and thereby established a well-defined set of vested interests. Developments in the field suggest that the CUE programs had some demonstration effect. For example, although the initial set of departments offering Ph.D. programs in the field were supported by CUE, many other departments initiated programs thereafter.

The Committee also recognized that conferences were an effective way to improve both the intellectual and the institutional bases of a field. Spirited, stimulating discussion can generate cohesion and recognition of common purpose, as well as produce useful ideas, and conference proceedings can contribute to the emerging literature. Because it is often very difficult to obtain financial support for conferences, the CUE program met a need that might otherwise have been neglected.

The approach of the Committee was experimental. Its flexible, evolving program tested new elements and moved on the basis of feedback information. Successful operations (and the people who carried them out) received further support. Unsuccessful operations were analyzed and, if further effort appeared unpromising, were quickly abandoned. In short, the CUE learning process was essentially a form of dynamic economizing.

The remainder of this report expands on these themes and documents them. Some valuations appear; given the broad overview attempted, some attempts at evaluation seemed justified, despite the inherent difficulties involved.

COVERAGE OF THE REPORT

The body of this report deals with dominant issues. Both the intellectual content and the institutional organization of the field are considered, though the emphasis is on the latter phase. Under the heading of intellectual content, some aspects of definition and classification are discussed. Then, some leading issues in urban economic thought are noted. The institutional organization of the field is discussed as follows: first, the state of university work in the field is surveyed, with primary focus on Ph.D. programs in urban economics; and then, the work of CUE is summarized, noting its purposes, strategies, and accomplishments. While CUE was one of a number of organizations promoting the development of the field, the documentation that follows demonstrates that its efforts were among the earliest and that their impact was substantial. Finally, an attempt is made to peer into the future; forecasts and prognoses are developed for both intellectual and institutional bases.

Appendixes are directed to specialized audiences interested in greater detail. They document the narrative and supply detailed information on those aspects of the field of particular concern to us here. The appendixes are divided into three parts: Part 1, "The Subject Matter of Urban Economics"—

Appendix A; Part 2, "The State of the Institutional Base"—Appendixes B and C; and Part 3, "The History of the Committee on Urban Economics"—Appendixes D through M.

Appendix A amplifies the discussion of the intellectual content of the field through a summary of the published proceedings[1] of the final CUE conference, which was devoted to developing an overview of the state of the field, in terms of subject matter.

Appendixes B and C focus on the present institutional base. Appendix B presents evidence on the growth and recognition of the field. (For example, the American Economic Association and the National Science Foundation have recently recognized urban economics as an area of specialization in a revised classification of economics as a discipline.) Urban economics programs for the doctorate are discussed in detail in Appendix C, which is based on a sample survey carried out for this report. A questionnaire was sent to 149 university departments offering the doctorate in economics or business administration. Response was good, and the results are discussed in some detail.

In the third part of the appendixes, detailed evidence is presented on the history of CUE. This report on expenditures, endeavors, and results provided an initial motivation for the present study. Given an expenditure of well over a million dollars and the need for a final accounting to the donor, the Ford Foundation, a detailed report was due. But in the process of relating benefits to costs, it soon became clear that the report would be of greater value, both to the Ford Foundation and to the more general audience of those concerned with the field,[2] if it were embedded in a wider frame.

The detailed story of CUE presents the institutional history and bookkeeping accounts for a specific organization. Beyond that, it names and credits some of the pioneers in the field, serves as a guide to some of the important literature and communication devices, and demonstrates techniques and strategies used in a successful experiment in academic innovation.

Intellectual Content of the Field

DEFINITION AND CLASSIFICATION

Jacob Viner argued that economics is what economists do.[3] As a corollary, it can be argued that urban economics is what urban economists do. Urban

---

1. Harvey S. Perloff and Lowdon Wingo, Jr., eds., *Issues in Urban Economics* (The Johns Hopkins Press for Resources for the Future, 1968).

2. This general audience is seen as including economists who are now or potentially concerned with work in the field, scholars concerned with urban problems from the vantage of other disciplines who are interested in the interface with urban economics, and administrators and historians of knowledge interested in academic innovations. Since the bulk of the audience is seen as coming from the first group, some technical material has been included.

3. This can be viewed as a compact statement of the nominalism of modern science,

4

economics can and will mean different things to different people, although available evidence suggests some trend toward a general consensus on the meaning and content of the field.

In practice, the field of urban economics has proved to be a useful way of organizing knowledge. It is useful because many important decisions fall within the area of study of its practitioners. Perloff and Wingo have spelled out some of the problem areas and policy issues generating interest and work in the field.[4] These include: (1) the economic growth and stagnation of cities, which has prompted studies of local economies; (2) the local impact of national policies and expenditures, such as defense spending; (3) developments in transportation, involving expressway construction and attendant metropolitan transportation studies; (4) urban public services and finance; and (5) urban development policy, including urban renewal, new town development, and policies addressed to urban poverty, crime, and other social problems.

Again, urban economics is useful because interrelationships among the components of the field can best be recognized and analyzed as part of a system. Thus, urban land utilization, urban transportation, and urban property tax and zoning policies are best viewed as comprising a subsystem within the general system of the urban economy.

Urban economics, as a field, is related to city and regional planning, and to geography, political science, and sociology as they concern themselves with the city. But though related in content and in application to these fields, it appears much more useful for urban economics to retain its autonomy as a subdiscipline of economics, rather than become a component of a subject matter labeled urban studies. This follows from the advantages of specialization, for the economist qua economist can bring to bear a highly developed set of theoretical constructs and methodological tools.

Within the discipline of economics, the field is closely related to local government finance, transportation economics, real estate economics, land economics, and regional economics. (These fields, too, are constructs developed because of utility in organizing knowledge.)

Not too long ago, regional and urban economics were viewed as a joint field. This was reasonable in the light of the limited development of, and participation in, both fields. For example, in a 1963 survey article in the *American Economic Review*, John R. Meyer included metropolitan studies within the purview of regional economics, though he noted that urban problems were playing an increasingly dominant role in regional analysis.[5] (The program at Resources for the Future entitled Regional Studies was retitled Regional and

---

in which definitions and classifications are not true or false but, rather, are more or less convenient and useful.

4. Perloff and Wingo, eds., *Issues in Urban Economics*, pp. 1-3.

5. John R. Meyer, "Regional Economics: A Survey," *American Economic Review* (March 1963), pp. 21, 27.

Urban Studies in 1963.) In the last few years, the urban phase appears to have gained enough momentum, in terms of literature and of participants, to spin off in its own right. Thus, pioneer university departments in the field generally label their course offerings "regional and urban economics," while the latest entrants label theirs "urban economics."

With the emergence and establishment of a new field, existing fields related to it tend to grow in its direction. Thus, state and local public finance develops a metropolitan public finance offshoot, and real estate programs evolve into "real estate and urban economics" programs.

Some aspects of the processes at work can be seen in Table 1, which shows the distribution of university courses defined as falling within the field of urban economics by those departments that offered the field for the doctorate in 1968. It seems clear that business school programs represent an extension or evolution of programs in real estate and land economics. In economics departments, urban economics courses, per se, accounted for one-third of all course offerings in the field as defined by the departments. Urban-regional and regional courses comprised about the same fraction, while the remaining one-third were cataloged under the headings of location theory, metropolitan finance, housing, transportation, etc.

It can be seen from Table 1 that the question of definition and classification can be posed as: What do people generally include within the field of urban economics?

A review of university course descriptions yields a number of common themes, which can be aggregated into a universal course description:

Nature, function, and economic foundation of cities. Resource allocation in an urban context. Sources of suboptimality. Urban economic growth. Loca-

Table 1. Distribution of University Courses Defined as Falling within the Field of Urban Economics (1968)

Subject	Economics departments	Business schools
Urban economics	36	10
Urban land and real estate economics	1	27
Location theory	9	3
Urban-regional economics	25	4
Regional economics	12	0
Metropolitan and local public finance[a]	13	0
All other[b]	14	9
Total	110	53

[a] Includes public investment decision making.

[b] Includes: housing (4); transportation (2); urban studies (6); urban geography (3); methods (4); human resources and labor (3); welfare economics (1).

Source: Replies by university departments offering the doctorate in urban economics to a questionnaire survey carried out for this report.

tion of population and economic activity. Spatial structure and organization. Land use. Central business district functions. Centralizing and decentralizing forces. Urban public services. Government decision making in metropolitan areas. Housing, transportation, racial discrimination, poverty problems, pollution.

In its first grant period (1959-64), CUE recognized five core areas in the field:

1. *Structure and growth of the urban economy.* The city is viewed in its role as a component of the national economy—an element in a national system of cities. Problems of city growth and decline are classified under this head.

2. *Intrametropolitan organization and change.* This subfield focuses on the spatial dimension of the metropolitan economy, in terms of the organization of economic activities within the metropolis and the relation of city form and the allocation of resources. Land use, urban housing, and urban transportation are specific topics of interest.

3. *Urban public services and welfare.* This area involves concern with the urban public economy, addressing problems associated with efficient allocation of public resources and the interaction of the public and private sectors. Topics covered include federal, state, and local finance in a metropolitan context and the demand for and supply of urban public services.

4. *Economics of urban human resources* (originally labeled "Population and human ecology"). Focal topics are households as suppliers of labor services in urban labor markets and urban populations as consumers of final products of the economy. In particular, there is concern with the plight of the urban Negro confronting labor and housing markets constrained by discrimination. Migration, poverty, and investment in human capital (including education) are examined in an urban context.

5. *Regional accounts.* The systematic organization of flows of information needed for regional economic analysis is the focus of this core area. The urban region is the relevant unit for urban economics application. (The usual unit is the SMSA—the Standard Metropolitan Statistical Area—but other units will be useful in some contexts.)

This topical organization can be seen to evolve from three sources: (1) an attempt to attain closure; that is, to achieve essentially complete coverage of topics that the CUE membership saw as germane; (2) an attempt to attain balance, giving each problem area roughly the same level of importance; and (3) an attempt to reflect underlying areas of specialization from which urban economics emerged. Some of the subfields were relatively undeveloped, but work in them appeared vital in terms of policy needs (the economics of urban discrimination, for example).

These subfields have grown at different rates. In particular, the area of urban human resource economics has lagged when compared to growth in the other subfields. To some extent, this reflects the rise of a specialty in human resource economics, with a focus embracing the entire economy, and with results hopefully applicable to urban economic problems. But it also reflects the lack of development of group cohesion among researchers concerned with specific topics under this heading. Labor economists, consumption economists, human ecologists, and fledgling human resource economists have rather diverse points of view, so that communication was (and is) difficult. Although CUE attempted to establish communication links among leading scholars in the emerging subfield, little cohesion and community of interest appeared.

Some broad generalizations on the field of urban economics seem germane at this point. (1) The field is anything but static; continuous evolution and redefinition can be expected over time. (2) The field is fashionable *because* it is viable and has considerable growth potential. Older, more established fields are relating and reorganizing with respect to urban economics, so that a student in the field will be following a specific current within the broad stream of economic thought. (3) Because of its growth characteristics, work in the field probably yields some significant spillovers; some of the advances are of use in other areas of economics and in other social sciences.

SOME LEADING ISSUES

A sense of the intellectual content of the field of urban economics can be obtained from a discussion of some leading issues.[6]

First, there is concern with why some urban areas are richer, more egalitarian, or more stable in income; why there are differential growth rates in income and population; and whether there are economies or diseconomies of city size. The available evidence indicates that the level, distribution, and stability of income in an urban area are functions of its industry mix. Large urban areas have generally acquired a capacity to innovate and introduce growth industries, reflecting strong service sectors, infrastructure, and universities. There is a filtering-down process, as older, established industries tend to shift from large areas to smaller areas where labor is less skilled and cheaper. Economies and diseconomies of size tend to balance, so that large cities will probably grow at the same rate as the national average.

A second issue concerns the role and function of the city. The city exists because it effectively performs economic functions in both a production and a consumption context. The underlying rationale for the city may well be that of providing close, easy, and multifarious contact so that decision units may interact in fruitful ways. Access is a key organizing principle; the pattern of development in urban areas is a function of access. Population density, economic activity, and land value decline from the center, for the center is the point of maximum accessibility—things and persons can be assembled here at

---

6. See Appendix A for a more detailed treatment and for source citations.

minimum cost. The existence of high speed transport routes with limited points of access leads to some modification of the pattern, with some clustering and uneven density decline.

The city may also be viewed as an upgrading mechanism; inmigrants can improve their economic status as a consequence of their migration to the city. Although continued inmigration of the rural poor keeps neighborhoods poor, the people become better off. Recent arrivals improve their lot relative to their rural origin; less recent inmigrants generally improve their lot over time and move to richer neighborhoods.

Finally, there are a set of issues around the theme of the suburbs versus the central city and the argument that fragmented local government ought to be replaced by metropolitan-wide government. But there are difficulties. The suburbs will resist such a development strongly, because richer communities with a higher tax base tend to have lower tax rates. Again, fragmentation can reflect differences in consumer preferences for public services. And last, available evidence on costs suggests that governments serving 50,000 to 100,000 persons are most efficient. In consequence, it is likely that the governmental response to metropolitan growth will increasingly occur at the federal level.

Institutional Organization of the Field

THE STATE OF UNIVERSITY PROGRAMS

In this report, a reading on the institutional state of the field is furnished primarily by information on departments offering the doctorate in urban economics.[7] As noted earlier, this makes sense in terms of the locus of intellectual capital in the field; the departmental programs involved can be viewed as the productive plant that will produce most of the new professionals.

In 1968, as part of this study, a survey questionnaire was sent to the 149 university departments in the United States that offered the doctorate in economics or business administration.[8] Of the 145 departments that replied to the questionnaire, fifty-three stated that they had, or would be introducing next year, a program in urban economics as a field of specialization for the doctorate. The distribution of responses is summarized in Table 2.

The recent development of the field can be illustrated by the distribution of years in which economics departments[9] established urban economic

---

7. Appendix B presents evidence on growth and recognition of the field. Appendix C is an extended version of the present discussion of doctoral programs.

8. The term "department" is used here in a generic sense to cover both departments of economics and business schools; the latter term, in turn, covers graduate schools of business administration, colleges of business, etc.

9. Schools of business are not included because the establishment dates they listed often referred to real estate programs, rather than to urban economics programs. One business school distinguished between the two, listing 1959 for the establishment of its urban real estate program, and 1968 for its urban economics program.

Table 2. Programs in Urban Economics by Department (1968)

Questionnaire response	Economics departments	Business schools	All
With program			
Have program now	30	12	42
Will introduce next year	10[a]	1	11
	—	—	—
Total with program	40	13	53
No program	57	35	92
No response to questionnaire	1	3	4
	—	—	—
Grand total	98	51	149

[a] Of these, nine departments were to introduce the program in 1969, one in 1968. Presumably, the latter case involved the academic, rather than calendar, year.

Source: Appendix Table C-2.

Table 3. Dates of Establishment of Doctoral Programs in Urban Economics by Departments of Economics

Year	Number of departments introducing field
1969	9
1968	7
1967	5
1966	5
1965	2
1964	4
1963	2
1962	1
1961	3
1960	1
1959	1

Source: Appendix Table C-4.

programs, as shown in Table 3. It can be concluded that there is an accelerating trend in the introduction of the field.

In an evaluation of the quality of departments of economics in universities in the United States based on combined samples of department chairmen, senior scholars, and junior scholars, the American Council on Education rated thirty-six departments as above average in quality.[10] Table 4 relates specific quality classifications to the establishment of doctoral programs in urban economics and indicates that departments rated above average are more likely to have introduced the field, perhaps reflecting a propensity to innovate. In terms of percentage, 58 per cent of the higher quality departments have pro-

10. Allan M. Cartter, *An Assessment of Quality in Graduate Education* (American Council on Education, 1966).

Table 4. Quality of Economics Department Related to Establishment of Program in Urban Economics (1968)

	Number of departments	
Quality of economics department	Have program in field	Do not have program
Departments rated above average in quality of graduate faculty		
Distinguished	5	2
Strong	5	4
Good	6	7
Adequate plus	5	2
	—	—
Subtotal, rated above average	21	15
All other departments	19	43
	—	—
Grand total	40	58

Sources: Allan M. Cartter, *An Assessment of Quality in Graduate Education* (American Council on Education, 1966), pp. 34-38, and sample survey, this report. See also Appendix Table C-3.

Table 5. Faculty Participation in Forty-Four University Programs in Urban Economics (1968)

Department category	Full-time equivalent man-years			Number of persons involved
	Teaching	Research	All	
Economics departments	34.0	42.0	76.0	136
Business schools	16.5	15.8	32.3	50
	—	—	—	—
Total	50.5	57.8	108.3	186

Source: Appendix Table C-6.

grams, as opposed to 30 per cent of all other departments. The difference is statistically significant. Within the higher quality group, the highest and lowest rated subgroups have a greater tendency to introduce the field than do the middle subgroups, but differences are not statistically significant.

Questionnaire responses from thirty-eight of forty-two departments with programs now in effect,[11] and six of eleven departments introducing the field next year, furnish detailed information about the characteristics of university programs in urban economics. Data on faculty participation in teaching and research in urban economics appears in Table 5 in terms both of full-time

11. Of the forty-two departments with programs now in effect, thirty-eight completed the questionnaire; one did not furnish information; and three had collaborative programs with other departments, with the latter making the major contribution to the program.

equivalent man-years (two half-years equal one man-year) and of persons involved. (In the latter category, two persons with a half-year each in the field equal two persons.) In terms both of full-time equivalent man-years and of persons, 70 per cent of the faculty participating in programs in urban economics were in departments of economics and 30 per cent were in business schools. Table 6 shows the average faculty participation for departments with programs in the field. Business schools had somewhat higher levels of participation than departments of economics (with 5.3 man-years versus 4.2 man-years). Table 7 shows that of the 163 courses cataloged in the field, 132 furnished graduate credit; roughly two-thirds of the total annual enrollment of approximately thirty-five hundred was in courses for graduate credit.

Table 8 presents data on the number of participants in the educational phase of programs in urban economics, in terms of postdoctoral, doctoral, and pre-

Table 6. Average Faculty Participation Per Department, for Forty-Four Departments with Programs in Urban Economics (1968)

Department category	Full-time equivalent man-years			Number of persons
	Teaching	Research	All	
Economics departments	1.04	1.32	2.36	4.2
Business schools	1.75	1.67	3.42	5.3

Source: Appendix Table C-7.

Table 7. Numbers of Courses and Enrollment in Forty-Four Programs in Urban Economics

Course type	Number of courses (1968)	Annual course enrollment (average 1967-68)
Undergraduate credit only	31	1,145
Graduate credit	132	2,359
Total	163	3,504

Source: Appendix Table C-9.

Table 8. Number of Persons Enrolled in the Educational Phase of Programs in Urban Economics (1968)

Category	Number
Postdoctoral Fellows (1966-68)	21
Persons awarded doctorates (1963-68)	70[a]
Doctoral candidates	90[a]
Precandidacy students	288[a,b]

[a] There is some understatement because some departments did not list numbers.

[b] Includes 174 in economics, forty in business administration, and seventy-four in all other fields.

Source: Appendix Table C-12.

12

doctoral status. The CUE policy of encouraging young scholars to follow lines of research suggested by their dissertations is reflected by the fact that, of the twenty-one postdoctoral fellows, twenty received support from CUE programs.

Table 9 lists sources of support for doctorates completed from 1963 through 1968 and for doctorates in progress in 1968. (In several cases there was more than one source of support for a given doctorate, so that totals are greater than those in Table 8.) Table 10 summarizes sources of support for current departmental research. The Committee on Urban Economics was an important source of support for both doctorates and departmental research.

In the survey questionnaire, a number of possible problems was listed and respondents were asked to indicate those that applied to their programs. The problems were structured in terms of discerned shortages. (Of course, this involves value judgments regarding levels of adequacy.) A problem noted is labeled a "complaint" for ease of exposition. Table 11 lists the number of complaints, by category. Shortage of funds was the most common complaint,

Table 9. Sources of Support for the Doctorate in Urban Economics (1968)

Source	Completed doctorates (1962-68)	Doctorates in progress (1968)	Total
CUE	17	27	44
University	22	22	44
Federal government	7	9	16
State and local government	4	2	6
Foundations	8	10	18
Research institutes, etc.	4	1	5
Self-support	1	4	5
Not listed	11	18	29
Totals[a]	74	93	167

[a] Totals exceed figures in Table 8 because several doctorates had more than one source of support.

Source: Appendix Table C-13.

Table 10. Sources of Support for Current Departmental Research (1968)

Source of support	Number of departmental programs receiving support
CUE	10
Other RFF	5
University and university agencies	7
Federal government	18
State government	5
Foundations	12
Research institutes, etc.	3

Source: Appendix Table C-14.

13

Table 11. Complaints by Departments (1968)

Item seen to be in short supply	Number of complaints registered
Funds	25
Faculty	20
Qualified students	15
Good teaching materials	10
Positions for successful doctoral candidates	0
Other[a]	2

[a] Good research: 1; good data: 1.
Source: Appendix Table C-16.

followed in descending order by shortages of faculty, qualified students, and good teaching materials. No department foresaw too few positions available for students successfully completing their doctoral work, indicating a general feeling that demand in the field was strong, and will continue to be strong for some time to come.

In sum, the available evidence suggests a large expansion in capacity in departmental programs and in the supply of economists in the field. This has occurred in a relatively short span of time, and a great deal of the growth has taken place in the last few years. There have been and are other sources of supply: urban economists in departments without a program in the field or not granting the doctorate, urban economists outside the universities, and economists migrating into urban economics from other fields in the discipline.

Nevertheless, the increment by way of institutionalized programs appears quite significant, and the upward trend seems likely to continue. From this vantage, it seems likely that increases in demand will keep pace with (if not move ahead of) these supply increases.

THE ACTIVITIES OF THE COMMITTEE ON URBAN ECONOMICS[12]

In 1958, no department of economics offered a Ph.D. program in urban economics and, hence, no formally constituted institutional base existed in the universities when Harvey Perloff set forth the idea of a committee to help promote the development of the field, with a focus on university activity.[13] With the support of RFF executive officers Reuben G. Gustavson and Joseph L. Fisher, Perloff worked with officials of the Ford Foundation to transform the basic notion into an action program through a series of planning papers and conferences. The proposed form and objectives of the committee were developed, and in February 1959 RFF submitted a formal proposal to the Ford Foundation. The major purposes of the proposed committee would be to:

12. Detailed information on the Committee and its activities appears as appendixes D through M.

13. Harvey Perloff certainly would appear in any roll of the Founding Fathers of the field.

14

- develop university centers in urban economics;
- attract new talent into the field;
- serve a clearing house function;
- sponsor conferences;
- assist in specific metropolitan studies;
- promote data improvement; and
- serve a liaison function.

RFF would serve as fiscal agent and provide the secretariat for the committee.

The Ford Foundation acted favorably on the grant request, and in July 1959 announced a five-year grant of $375,000 to RFF to establish an interuniversity group to advance research and education in urban economics. A number of leading economists who were interested in the field were contacted and agreed to serve.[14] Lowdon Wingo first served as Committee secretary, and later was invited to join the Committee. At the first meeting, in October 1959, the name "Committee on Urban Economics" was selected. The acronym, CUE, was a natural consequence.

Early in 1960 the state of university activity was assessed by means of a questionnaire survey, and it was concluded that "education and research in the field of urban economics was in an embryonic stage. . . ."[15]

In a letter written in 1960, Harvey Perloff appraised the prospects and potential role of CUE in the following fashion:

I look at the future of CUE with quite a bit of optimism. I see CUE as being essentially an intellectual and organizational experiment. If the experiment works out well, it means that we will have developed what may well be a truly significant arrangement for getting an important academic job done. It would mean that we worked out an effective way for combining the strength of a research outfit, of personally-involved university people, and of foundation funds. . . .

If the Committee turns out to be a failure—if it falls apart after a while—I still believe we will have learned some useful things, and we will have given some sort of boost to the field of urban economics. Frankly, I don't see why this need happen as long as we are willing to permit the membership of the Committee to change. . . .

If the Committee functions at all well, within a period of 5 to 10 years the field of urban economics ought to be where most fields are after 20 or 30 years. This I would see as an appropriate test of success (although I appreciate the difficulty of measuring this sort of thing).[16]

During the first grant period two advisory committees were set up: the Committee on Urban Public Expenditures (COUPE) and the Committee on Urban Human Resources. A third, the Committee on Regional Accounts

14. Detailed information on Committee membership appears as Appendix E.
15. Minutes of the Committee on Urban Economics, meeting of January 28, 1960, p. 2.
16. Letter from Harvey S. Perloff to Harold J. Barnett, February 3, 1960.

(CORA), had been established prior to the organization of CUE, and was separately financed. However, CORA quickly became associated with CUE and worked closely with the latter Committee after its establishment. Each of the three advisory committees developed programs and held conferences in conjunction with CUE.[17]

The Committee's work in the first period had an exploratory focus; by the end of that period it was ready and able to shift its emphasis to promoting the expansion of the institutional base. A proposal was made to the Ford Foundation for a five-year program, again under the auspices of RFF, to strengthen university capabilities in urban economics. The Foundation again acted favorably and a grant of $900,000 was awarded in September 1964. The award was explicitly set up as a terminal grant, so that at the end of the grant period, the sponsorship of CUE by RFF would be terminated. It was felt that fledgling activities helped during the grant period ought to have developed momentum of their own by the end of the period.

Although the Committee had always defined the focus of its interest and activities as falling within the field of economics, it recognized the importance of the interface between the field and other social science disciplines. It thus included representatives of those disciplines in its membership from 1960 onward, and increased their representation with a general increase in membership at the start of the second grant period. This facilitated an expanded set of activities by the Committee.

The major means employed to strengthen the institutional base was a program of matching grants to universities. During the organization of that program, Wilbur Thompson served as director of the Committee for a one-year period in 1964. A period of research at RFF by Thompson, also sponsored by CUE, eventuated in his pioneering book, A Preface to Urban Economics,[18] which has found wide use as a text in the field.

In 1967-68, the membership of the Committee was again expanded. Five of the eight new members were key persons at the matching grant universities; all, in a sense, represented a new wave of urban economists. The expansion of the Committee helped in assessing the role of a successor committee as a link between university centers. Some co-ordination of university activities, a basic goal throughout the life of CUE, would thus continue. With the completion of the activities of CUE, the successor committee was organized under the chairmanship of Dick Netzer.

In addition to Harvey Perloff, as CUE chairman, eight persons served throughout the entire life of the Committee. They are: Harold J. Barnett, Joseph L. Fisher, Walter W. Heller, Werner Z. Hirsch, Edgar M. Hoover, Richard Ruggles, Arthur M. Weimer, and Lowdon Wingo. Lyle Fitch and

17. Detailed information on advisory committees appears as Appendix F.

18. Wilbur Thompson, A Preface to Urban Economics (The Johns Hopkins Press for Resources for the Future, 1965).

16

Howard Schaller joined the Committee in 1960, and served on it thereafter. Of the thirty-two persons who served on CUE at one time or another, twenty-three were from the fields of economics and business administration, and nine were from other social science disciplines.

During the ten years of its existence under RFF auspices, CUE spent 1.37 million dollars, consisting of the Ford Foundation grants and accrued interest thereon. Program spending can be classified under the following headings:

- Research grants,
- Communication grants,
- Conferences,
- The fellowship program,
- The matching grant program,
- Terminal grants.

Let us examine each in turn.[19]

Research grants. CUE supported twenty-one research projects, of which seventeen were at universities, two at research institutes, and two within RFF. As of late 1968, most of the projects had eventuated in published results or in manuscripts moving through the review process.

A critical review of the files of research fund requests and grants reveals both risk preference and risk aversion in the Committee's decisions. Preference for risk was shown in the tendency to encourage work by newcomers in the field. Generally, the grants in these cases were relatively small, though a few were substantial. Aversion to risk appears in the case of grants supporting work by established practitioners; support generally was extended only to work that appeared to have especially good prospects. In these cases grant requests generally were relatively large.

This behavior can be explained as reflecting two distinct goals: the encouragement of participation in the field as against the production of scholarly work. Although the strategies employed might then be rationalized, in retrospect a case can be made for a higher tolerance for risk in the funding of research by established practitioners.

Communication grants. A major CUE goal was the improvement of the supply of information in the field. In line with this, seven grants were made for surveys of the field (or part of it), or for setting up information services of use to scholars in the field. Results of supported activities have included three conferences, a series of seminars in urban public finance, three surveys and

19. Each topic is treated in detail in an appendix, as follows: research grants, Appendix H; communication grants, Appendix I; conferences, Appendix J; the fellowship program, Appendix K; and the matching grant program, Appendix L. Appendix D is a chronology, while Appendix G summarizes expenditures and Appendix M lists participants in CUE programs.

reports of research needs, and three periodicals supplying information on the field. The periodicals were the *Research Digest,* reporting on research projects under way; a newsletter, *News in Urban Economics;* and a graduate student journal of reviews of literature in the field, *Reviews in Urban Economics.* Experience with the periodicals was mixed. The *Research Digest,* published by the Bureau of Community Planning, University of Illinois, was in existence prior to the CUE grant and is now firmly established. Its scale of operations was recently expanded on the basis of a Ford Foundation grant. The newsletter and graduate student journal were experimental endeavors which showed promise but were not successfully established as continuing publications. The experience with them should be of use in any similar publication ventures by the successor committee to CUE.

Conferences. The Committee and its related advisory committees organized a series of conferences to further the development of urban economics. In many cases, conference proceedings were subsequently published under RFF auspices. (See Table 12 for titles.) These include one publication on urban human resources, two on urban public expenditures, and three on regional accounts. The final CUE conference was devoted to an overview of the entire field, and led to the publication of two volumes, one concerned with revenue sharing and the city and the other with major themes and directions in urban economics.

The Fellowship Program. The CUE fellowship program consisted of grants-in-aid to doctoral candidates who were writing their dissertations in the field.

Table 12. Published Proceedings of Conferences of the Committee on Urban Economics and its Advisory Committees

Subfield or field	Date of conference	Title, editor of published volume, and publication date
Urban human resources	1962	*Human Resources in the Urban Economy,* ed. Mark Perlman (1963)
Urban public expenditures	1962	*Public Expenditure Decisions in the Urban Community,* ed. Howard A. Schaller (1963)
	1964	*The Public Economy of Urban Communities,* ed. Julius Margolis (1965)
Regional accounts	1960	*Design of Regional Accounts,* ed. Werner Hochwald (1961)
	1962	*Elements of Regional Accounts,* ed. Werner Z. Hirsch (1964)
	1964	*Regional Accounts for Policy Decisions,* ed. Werner Z. Hirsch (1966)
Urban economics	1967	*Revenue Sharing and the City,* ed. Harvey S. Perloff and Richard P. Nathan (1968) *Issues in Urban Economics,* ed. Harvey S. Perloff and Lowdon Wingo, Jr. (1968)

Interested university departments were invited to nominate one candidate per year; awards were based on an estimate of the applicant's ability to produce scholarly research and on the significance to the field of the proposed study. Nominated candidates enclosed an example of their scholarly writing with their application. Although initially limited to departments of economics and business schools, the program was soon extended to include other disciplines, if the candidate had an adequate grounding in graduate economics and his topic was germane to urban economics.

Fellowships were awarded in support of thirty-nine dissertations; of these, the doctorate was obtained in twenty-five cases, three dissertations were discontinued, and eleven presumably are still in progress. A check with university departments in late 1968 yielded evaluations of good progress for seven of the eleven cases in progress, anticipating completion within the year.

The sources of new entrants to the field can be inferred from the CUE fellowship awards. Of the thirty-nine fellowships, twenty-two went to departments that now have a doctoral program in urban economics; nine to departments of economics without a program; and eight to departments other than economics or business administration, including three each in planning fields and in regional science, and one each in geography and industrial administration.

An attempt was made to contact the twenty-five successful candidates regarding their postdoctoral experience. Information on twenty of the former Fellows shows that they have published three books and forty-two articles, monographs, or reports based on their doctoral dissertations, and that 58 per cent of their present work time, on the average, is devoted to urban economics. The Fellows were invited to attend the final CUE conference, and the general reaction was that they found the experience meaningful, both personally and professionally.

The Matching Grant Program. This program, initiated in 1965, was the concrete implementation of a shift to institution-building, the keynote of CUE endeavors in its second grant period. The goal of the matching grant program was to strengthen university teaching and research through the support of university centers in urban economics. A special feature of that program was a system of postdoctoral fellowships, seen by the Committee as an effective way of retaining newly developed professionals within the field. The kind of stress placed on this feature is something of an innovation, and is an example of a successful experiment or learning process carried out by CUE, imbedded in the broader experiment of the matching grant program.

The major elements of the program were:

1. CUE would recommend to RFF a grant of $75,000 to a qualified university for a program in urban economics if the university would match this with $125,000. The normal flow of funds would be $25,000 annually from each

source; thus, the CUE funds would continue for three years and the university's for five. It was hoped that the program would establish its worth by the end of the five-year period and that it would then be financed on a continuing basis by the university.

2. The university's program would be under way (or imminent) and would involve both organized research in urban economics and the availability of the field for the doctorate in economics or business administration. The university would make a firm commitment to support education and research in the field. Several faculty members, including at least one full-time senior member, would take part in the program, so that continuity would be assured. Finally, work in urban affairs would be available in other departments of the university.

University departments deemed potentially interested and capable of carrying out the program were contacted. Those responding favorably were invited to make a detailed application. Of those making applications, only five departments met all the requisite conditions. Full matching grants were made to these departments in 1966. These "major grant" departments were: the departments of economics at the University of California, Los Angeles; Washington University, St. Louis; Wayne State University; and Syracuse University; and the Graduate School of Business at Indiana University.

Over the next two years, additional matching grants were made to five departments that did not meet the grant conditions fully, and hence were at an earlier stage of development. The CUE contributions to these "pilot grant" departments—the departments of economics at Brown University, the University of Chicago, Iowa State University, New York University, and the University of Pittsburgh—ranged from $15,000 to $45,000.

The ten departments receiving CUE grants account for a significant share of university activity in urban economics, viewing all doctoral programs in the field. Thus, in 1968, CUE-supported departments accounted for about one-quarter of both full-time equivalent faculty and faculty persons involved and offered sixty-two courses in the field, roughly 35 per cent of the total. Student course enrollment in these departments was about a third of the total. Over half of the doctorates completed between 1962 and 1968 and nearly 60 per cent of the doctorates under way are accounted for by these ten departments. Finally, during 1967-68, twenty of twenty-one postdoctoral Fellows were located in these departments.

Terminal Grants. In completing its mission, and its operation under RFF auspices, CUE made a series of terminal grants for the continuation of some major activities. These included a grant to establish a successor interuniversity committee, a grant for a successor organization to the Committee on Regional Accounts, and a grant for continuing activities of the Committee on Urban Public Economics (COUPE).

The successor committee to CUE has been established under the chairmanship of Dick Netzer. It will serve as a link between university centers, so that co-ordination of university activities will continue. A Conference on Regional Accounts, under the chairmanship of Werner Z. Hirsch, will function as the reconstituted successor organization to the Committee on Regional Accounts. The seminars of COUPE on research in urban public finance will continue under the chairmanship of Julius Margolis.

Summary Evaluations. A final review of CUE activities shows total expenditures of $1.37 million, distributed as follows: outside research grants, 18 per cent; communication grants, 4 per cent; fellowships, 12 per cent; the matching grant program, 37 per cent; compensation covering internal research, conferences, and the secretariat function, 21 per cent; and terminal grants for continuing activities, 8 per cent.

To hazard a retrospective and intuitive judgment, the ratio of benefits to the costs involved probably is satisfactorily high, as attested to by appendix material which furnishes detailed documentation.

The program's effectiveness can be related to a number of factors:

1. Stress was laid on centering activities within the discipline of economics on an intellectual level, and within departments of economics on an institutional level. Some reasons for this stress were: (a) a discerned lag in concern with urban problems by economics, relative to other disciplines; (b) a belief that the application of economic theory and methods (with some help from other disciplines) was more effective than the development and application of "urban studies"; and (c) a belief that departments of economics, as existing institutional units, furnished the proper locus for ongoing activities.

2. Members of the Committee came from varied organizational backgrounds and intellectual disciplines. As a consequence, specific proposals were subjected to scrutiny from diverse points of view, and agreement represented a broad consensus.

3. The secretariat function was carried out as a non-university activity, located at a research institution. This was a source of independence, afforded a good vantage for an overview of the field, and furnished continuity.

4. The terminal nature of the grant was clearly noted and welcomed, so that ongoing activities would have to fend for themselves with the completion of RFF sponsorship.

5. Program requirements were made quite explicit to potentially participating individuals and departments. There was clear definition and delimitation. Those not meeting the requirements were not supported, even in cases, for example, where the department involved had a great deal of prestige.

6. Although postdoctoral fellowships have been in existence elsewhere for many years, the large number of such fellowships instituted by CUE is something of an innovation. It is very difficult to attract established scholars into a new area such as urban economics; more can be accomplished, in terms of professional participation, by focus on scholars at their point of entry into the discipline.

CUE's experiment in academic innovation has turned out well. Despite some failures along the way, the overall effort was successful.

Most of the failures were relatively minor. For instance, some of the experimental publication ventures were not successful. Again, the Committee took a considerable time to decide that its support of research did not extend to furnishing a publication outlet for the research results.

Perhaps the one major disappointment was the limited progress in the subfield of urban human resources. However, it is not clear that this reflects too little effort on the part of the Committee. It may well have been that the times were not ripe.[20]

Given that CUE has been a successful experiment in academic innovation, it is clear that much depended on the flexibility, energy, enthusiasm, and good sense of the Committee and its chairman. It can be concluded that these attributes were available in good measure.

FUTURE PROSPECTS FOR THE FIELD

It appears that urban economics has attained the take-off point, in the developmental sense of being capable of self-sustaining growth. But it is worth pondering where it is taking off to, in terms of options, alternatives, and opportunities.

In peering into the future, the outline followed earlier is useful. Thus, we can ask "Whither?" with respect to (1) the intellectual content of the field and (2) its institutional organization, including the possible role of the successor committee to CUE.

Some specific examples of substantive research questions may be noted.[21] Thus, there is need for a location matrix that indicates which industries follow a given industry to a locality, and when. Urban economists have been slow to consider questions of urban design, in terms of the rational specification of activities by small area, involving the basic question of scattered versus compact development. Again, almost no work has been done on investment in human beings in a spatial context. In particular, development analysis for human resource problems of the urban Negro population might well be

20. See the earlier discussion of subfields in the section on definition and classification, and see George Stolnitz's independent evaluation of little progress in the area in Perloff and Wingo, eds., *Issues in Urban Economics,* as noted in Appendix A.

21. These examples draw on comments by Wilbur Thompson, Edgar Hoover, George Stolnitz, and Eric Lampard in Perloff and Wingo, eds., *Issues in Urban Economics.*

viewed as corresponding to the dual economy problem of low-income nations. Finally, in the longest of runs, economists have not yet come to grips with the secular process of urbanization itself, including the evolution of city systems, as such, and the long-run economic transformations brought about by urbanization.

Turning to the survey carried out for this report, about half of the university departments that replied to the questionnaire availed themselves of an opportunity to identify and discuss the field's most critical problems. Most of the comments were concerned with the intellectual content of the field. Several clusters of response occurred. In one, it was argued that work in the field was too problem-centered, too ad hoc, too shallow, too action oriented. More integrative efforts were needed. Here, two variants appeared: one stressed the utility of "traditional" location theory and regional growth analysis; the other called for further and deeper application of "mainstream" economic theory. Almost as many departments, however, stressed the immediate need to try to find practical solutions to the pressing problems in the urban economy.

A related issue concerns the question of interdisciplinary urban studies. At least half-a-dozen departments expressed interest in moving their program into interdisciplinary work. This interest is likely to be tied to concern with immediate problems, as opposed to concern with more theory and deeper research, presumably centered in economics, per se.

Clearly, some of these issues are of general concern in scientific inquiry and in the applications of its results. We are all aware of action programs that are mounted prematurely on an inadequate information base, and we also know that if we wait until the results are all in, we never act (nor publish our research results). So we economize. We make trade-offs among the values involved, reflecting our own set of resources (knowledge and abilities) and assessment of risks and preferences. Different people arrive at different points of reconciliation—hardly surprising in a viable field.

The Committee faced some of these conflicts early in its history and worked out its own set of reconciliations (as noted above): both intellectual and institutional activities would be centered in economics, with recognition of the contribution of other disciplines, and with awareness of the profound importance of policy problems.

As the field grows, a variety of solutions will be tried. This can be viewed in sanguine fashion as experimentation, or more cynically, perhaps, as product differentiation. Varying assessments will be made on the importance of different components of the field; for example, some will stress intraurban and others, interurban studies.[22]

A good deal of specialization and differentiation can be expected, then,

22. See John F. Kain's review of Wilbur Thompson's *Preface to Urban Economics*, in *Journal of the American Institute of Planners* (May 1966), pp. 186-88. Kain stresses intraurban relations as opposed to interurban.

both in subject matter and method. Some departments will focus on public decision making in metropolitan areas, others on the system of cities, still others on city spatial structure, and so on. Most assuredly, there will be much more work on urban human resources, with a good deal of emphasis on the economics of the ghetto. Some departments are moving into specialization in this area, and there is now a broad consensus that much more should have been done and much more needs doing.

Specialization becomes more likely, too, with the increase in the number of departments offering urban economics for the doctorate. If the present rate of introduction continues, half of all economics departments will offer the field by late 1970, and most will do so in a few more years. Business schools are not moving so quickly, but there are increases here, too. New entrants into the field include some of the larger, more prestigious departments. Such developments portend the drawing to a close of the pioneer era, and with it, the sense that the field is exotic and rare.

On the institutional level, the rapid growth in the number of university departments and stringent budget constraints at present pose serious problems of funding. Many of the newer departments in the field are concerned about difficulties in securing recognition and funding for the work of younger scholars; older, better established departments are concerned with continuity at present levels of activity and possible program expansion. Such concern is healthy, but can be overdone. Awareness of the field's importance is not limited to economists—and the awareness grows.

One institutional feature of interest is the relation of the field to the federal establishment. Consider, for example, the relation of an earlier applied field—agricultural economics—to the U.S. Department of Agriculture (USDA). Here, there is highly organized and well-developed support of university research by grants, by collection and dissemination of data, and by in-house USDA research. Parallel efforts by the Department of Housing and Urban Development, the Department of Transportation, and the Department of Health, Education, and Welfare might well be anticipated and worked toward in the field of urban economics. Again, the independent but federally aided Urban Institute might well have a profound impact on the field. Certainly, a great deal more needs to be done in development of basic data in the field, and this could best be done by federal agencies. As an example, there is need for a unified system of accounts for all cities, simultaneously, and such an undertaking clearly could best be handled on the national level.

With the growth of the field, more and better communication becomes necessary. Thus, the experimental graduate student publication *Reviews in Urban Economics* might point the way toward a full-fledged student journal comparable to the law reviews. More important, a specialized journal for professionals in the field deserves serious consideration. There is, of course, the danger that this will be attempted prematurely with inadequate funding, and will fail. But it seems more likely that there will be a ready market and that a journal of this kind would be an integrative and cohesive force in the field.

The implementation of some of these suggested innovations could become part of the program of the successor committee to CUE.

At this writing it appears that this committee will serve at the minimum as an important channel of communication for the university departments in the field. In many respects, those departments will be engaged in vigorous, if not ruthless, competition. But, in some program areas, joint activities may well be desirable. For instance, development of support for postdoctoral fellowships might well be carried out as a joint undertaking.

The continuing activity by successor committees to the Committee on Regional Accounts, and the Committee on Urban Public Economics might well be paralleled by an effective and innovative new committee on urban human resources. And the continuing research seminar approach might be tried in other areas of specialization. In line with this, and given the development of increased specialization foreseen above, the successor committee to CUE might generate support for specific lines of concentrated inquiry, rather than support for the field as a whole. Specialization might move beyond the categories noted above to such subjects as measurement of key parameters in the urban environment, policies and programs for the inner city, or education in an urban context. Committee efforts might then be directed to augmenting the funding operations of individual departments attempting to develop differentiated programs in depth.

In sum, successor committee functions will probably encompass:

1. Communication;
2. Establishment and further encouragement of communication devices, perhaps including a professional journal in the field;
3. Development of federal agency support;
4. Efforts to establish data series, primarily under federal agency auspices;
5. Efforts to develop support for some overall programs; e.g., postdoctoral fellowships;
6. Efforts to augment support for specialized program development.

The communication function seems particularly important. With the entry of many new departments into the field, there is clearly a need to open channels of communication between them and departments with well-established programs.

The completion of the work of CUE is a sign that the era of exploration and early settlement draws to an end—but a large domain, indeed, awaits development.

APPENDIXES

PART 1. THE SUBJECT MATTER OF URBAN ECONOMICS

Appendix A
A Sampling of Some Leading Issues in Urban Economics

The final conference of the Committee on Urban Economics was devoted to an overview of the field, and the conference papers effectively span the substantive content of the field. Hence, the conference proceedings, *Issues in Urban Economics*, furnishes a convenient primary source for a sampling of some leading issues.[1] The material will be organized in terms of the five core areas used by CUE to classify the content of the field: (1) structure and growth of the urban economy (interurban relations); (2) intrametropolitan organization and change; (3) the urban public economy; (4) urban human resources; and (5) regional accounts.

Structure and Growth of the Urban Economy (Interurban Relations)[2]

Initial systematic inquiry into interurban economic relations began in the 1920s with the export base concept: industries selling outside the local economy were seen as the exogenous source of economic activity within the area. Yet the local service sector and attendant infrastructure may well be enduring (basic) and the export sector (a particular set of manufactures, say), transitory. When time and size are introduced as variables, these viewpoints can be reconciled: the export sector is important in the short run, and for small cities; the local service sector increases in importance with city size, and in the longer run.

The level, distribution, and stability of income in an urban area are functions of its industry mix. An area introducing new industries will tend to attract and develop a labor force of above-average skills. Producer durable industries are the least stable over the business cycle, while consumer nondurables are the

---

1. A good selection of additional sources appears in the "Selected Readings" at the end of each paper in Harvey S. Perloff and Lowdon Wingo, Jr., eds., *Issues in Urban Economics* (The Johns Hopkins Press for Resources for the Future, 1968), hereafter cited as *Issues*.

2. The primary source for this section is Wilbur R. Thompson, "Internal and External Factors in the Development of Urban Economics," *Issues*, pp. 43-62. The section also draws on Eric E. Lampard, "The Evolving System of Cities in the United States: Urbanization and Economic Development," *Issues*, pp. 81, 93-94, 138.

most stable; however, there is some diffusion of area impact because non-durable industries tend to stand alone (for example, the textile town) while durable industries tend to cluster (reflecting external economies). In such clusters, diversified industries can have somewhat different cycles.

Although a growing percentage of output comes from multi-product, multi-plant corporations that are management controlled, the literature on the location of industry is based on one-plant, single-product, owner-controlled firms. The least-cost location for the multi-plant organizations is at or near a multiple-node transportation center, usually a large city.

Large size is generally accompanied by a diversified mix of exports, in terms of both income elasticities and age of industry. Because of this diversification, growth of the area will be neither very fast nor very slow. However, it is likely that large urban areas are biased somewhat toward growth industries (high income-elastic and/or new products), but that growth is dampened by the spinning-off of established industries. The large urban area has generally developed a capacity to innovate in acquiring new export bases. Hence, its long-term economic base is its service sector, infrastructure, and universities. In the later stages of a given industry, there is a filtering down of by now routinized functions to smaller, less skilled, and cheaper labor areas.

Larger places have clear and sizable advantages in cheaper transport and utilities, more skilled and varied labor force, and better education and research. There are some external diseconomies of size, but the most significant scarce factor may be urban public management. It seems likely, then, that national policy will be directed toward mastering the management of large clusters, rather than preventing growth above a specified size. In the long run, it is likely that economies and diseconomies of scale will balance out, so that large cities (over one million population) will grow at average rates.

The investigation of interurban relations can furnish an entry to the general historical problem of the interrelation of urbanization and economic change. In terms of the broad sweep of history, the urban transformation is a vital component of development. Thus, the urban transformation contributed to a progressive unfolding of the industrial system by way of declines in fertility, greatly increased specialization, and the development of a new socioeconomic structure, with a strong middle as well as working class.

Intrametropolitan Organization and Change[3]

Location theory is an important tool in both intercity and intracity analysis. In brief, location theory asserts that the cost of distance is the ordering element in the territorial distribution of economic activity.

The important exogenous determinants of location have been identified as: (1) topographic features, including the waterfront; (2) existing gateways to the

---

3. The primary source for this section is Edgar M. Hoover, "The Evolving Form and Organization of the Metropolis," *Issues,* pp. 237-84. The section also draws on Richard F. Muth, "Urban Residential and Housing Markets," *Issues,* pp. 285-333, and Britton Harris, "Quantitative Models of Urban Development: Their Role in Metropolitan Policy-Making," *Issues,* p. 394.

outside world (terminal locations); and (3) the focus of maximum overall accessibility. The last item refers to the place at which all persons could assemble with minimum total man-miles of travel. The focal point tends to be stable, though its relative cost advantage can change rapidly. In principle, there are a variety of points of this sort, depending on what (or whom) is being assembled with minimum cost. The significance of the focal point to an activity is a function of how dependent it is on access to the flow in question. Access considerations are involved in the mutual attraction between complementary parties: e.g., stores and customers, employees and firms, pupils and schools.

Indeed, the underlying rationale for the city may be seen as that of providing and facilitating close, easy, and multifarious contact, so that decision units may interact in fruitful and efficient ways. Agglomerative (or clustering) factors also include scale economies for the individual firm and external economies facing a group of firms on their factor and/or product markets. Then, from the center outward there is a density gradient where density is a negative function of radial distance. This holds not only for urban population density, but for a number of related variables, including land values.

Some special cases and some sources of change are noteworthy. Thus, some land uses with an off-center optimum location do better in concentrated single-center form (because of agglomeration economies) rather than in a ring pattern. Examples include airports and stadiums. The pattern of land development as a function of access depends on how travel time is related to distance. A close relation leads to a continuous pattern of development; while a limited number of fast routes with limited points of access leads to clustering and uneven density. Again, high-speed intercity transportation between city centers may promote new growth for central business districts. Finally, urban renewal can be evaluated as a costly and less than satisfactory means of altering urban structure.

Focusing on the urban housing market, it was traditionally believed that housing demand is inelastic with respect to income, yet recent work indicates an income elasticity of at least $+1$, and perhaps as large as $+2$. Racial segregation in housing expresses white community preferences, not those of real estate agents or landlords. There has been a great decline in substandard housing over time so that the growing concern about slums has paralleled great improvement in housing.

Higher-income households appear to have a stronger preference for space relative to access than do lower-income households. However, very high correlations among density, blight, obsolescence, and social status make it difficult to distinguish between the following hypotheses on consumer preferences for increased space versus the convenience of shortened travel:

1. a preference for low residential densities;
2. a preference for good housing conditions and neighborhood cleanliness;
3. a high-income group preference for segregation from low-income groups.

The median income level of census tracts increases with distance from the central business district. However, when age of dwelling unit is included in

31

the analysis, the income and distance association disappears. This suggests a high-income group preference for new housing rather than for low density. (Another important factor here is the stage of the family life cycle, since families with young children tend to have a strong preference for single-family housing.)

The Urban Public Economy[4]

Subnational government finance may be viewed in terms of stabilization, distribution, and allocation functions. In the past, subnational governments were usually fiscally perverse in their reaction to the business cycle. But since World War II the strong secular rise of state and local expenditures has over-whelmed the cyclical influence. With respect to distribution, the incidence of property and sales taxes relative to state and local expenditure benefits implies a significant redistribution in favor of the poor. But this occurs within jurisdictions, so that there is essentially no redistribution between the suburban rich and the central city poor. Finally, allocation dominates the provision and financing of public services at the local level, with three types of goods involved: (1) essentially private goods which are institutionally located in the public sector; (2) goods satisfying social wants, wherein the public sector attempts to satisfy consumers as if a market solution were obtainable, and (3) merit goods, wherein the individual receives more of the public services than the amount he would have purchased; e.g., he has more days of school than he would have paid for himself.

Because of real-world imperfections and externalities, and because of the absence of redistribution between suburbs and central city noted above, it is often argued that fragmented local governments ought to be replaced by metropolitan-area-wide government. But few prospects for change are to be found in the present pattern. The notorious resistance of the suburbs to metropolitan government is quite rational, given their favorable position: richer communities with higher tax bases tend to have lower tax rates. (Dispersive tendencies in the location of industry are reinforced by tax differentials working in the same direction.) Again, the fragmentation of government could well be a response to consumer demand for varied bundles of public services. While some economies of scale (and area-wide spillovers) occur for such items as air pollution control, sewage disposal, utilities, transportation, and planning; most other services—i.e., fire and police protection, libraries, parks, and education—exhibit little or no economies of scale. The available evidence on costs suggests that governments serving 50,000 to 100,000 persons are most efficient. In any event, the response to growing metropolitanism is increasingly occurring on the federal level, in line with reluctance to change fragmentation

---

4. The primary source for this section is Dick Netzer, "Federal, State, and Local Finance in a Metropolitan Context," *Issues*, pp. 435-78; in particular, pp. 435-46, 460. The section also draws on Julius Margolis, "The Demand for Urban Public Services," *Issues*, pp. 534, 542 and 546-47; Werner Z. Hirsch, "The Supply of Urban Public Services," *Issues*, pp. 509 and 517; and Alan K. Campbell and Jesse Burkhead, "Public Policy for Urban America," *Issues*, pp. 581 and 583-84.

32

through state or local action. In allocation, public services are often zero priced. Three forms of rationing arise in this situation: congestion, administrative rules, and an active market in other assets yielding access to the services in question. Often, urban public services are evaluated as inadequate when, in fact, the discerned inadequacy involves a focus on "needs" (at zero price) and a disregard of benefits.

Urban Human Resources[5]

Human resources, as a well-defined area of work in the discipline of economics, emerged in the early 1960s, embracing the "Population and human ecology" category set forth by CUE in 1959. Reviewing the work in this area, George Stolnitz concluded: "Theoretical work by the economist has been laggard in the human resource field at the national level, and conspicuously so in urban matters."[6]

Some relationships that have been established in the area may be noted. Urbanization, suburbanization, and Negro inmigration reflect very long-term trends. By 1920, 50 per cent of the population of the United States lived in cities. During each decade from 1900 to 1930, the percentage increase in urban population was greater than has been the case in any of the decades since 1940. Central city population relative to the metropolitan total peaked at two-thirds in the 1930s, and declined to 47 per cent in 1966; any central city increases now occur primarily through annexations. Rapid suburbanization has been going on for more than half a century. The central city Negro population has generally been increasing at an accelerating rate, in terms of long-term trends, but the historical acceleration may have slowed recently. Available evidence indicates that outmigration is largely a result of life-cycle events, and inmigration reflects economic opportunities. Negroes have a greater tendency to migrate to areas where friends and relatives are located, and they are less sensitive to job opportunities than white migrants. Negroes have much higher mortality and fertility rates than do whites; the death rate is 40 per cent higher and the life expectancy is 10 per cent lower. Higher fertility levels have Malthusian implications. In urban areas, as in the United States as a whole, Negro unemployment rates are twice those of whites.

In considering urban poverty, it is worth stressing that inmigration of the rural poor keeps neighborhoods poor, but the people change. "The city is a sort of 'sausage factory' at one end of which the poor enter and where, at the other end, many of them leave poor no more. . . ."[7] There has been a shift, of course, from foreign-born to native rural migrants.

There is growing support for the policy proposition that the neighborhood

---

5. The primary source for this section is George J. Stolnitz, "The Changing Profile of our Urban Human Resources," *Issues*, pp. 187-227; in particular, pp. 189-209. The section also draws on Oscar Ornati, "Poverty in the Cities," *Issues*, pp. 354 and 358; and Sidney Sonenblum, "The Uses and Development of Regional Projections," *Issues*, pp. 154-55.

6. Stolnitz, "The Changing Profile . . . ," *Issues*, p. 188.

7. Ornati, "Poverty in the Cities," *Issues*, p. 358.

itself ought to be regenerated, in a process similar to that of the economic development of underdeveloped countries. Economic redevelopment at the neighborhood level hinges on three assumptions: homogeneity of behavior of residents; the possibility of adopting "protectionist" policies; and the existence of significant levels of unused resources. Some evidence supports these assumptions. (For example, poverty neighborhoods have significant internal cash flows—including welfare and income from illegal activities—which could be rechanneled.)

Regional Accounts

Work on regional accounts has focused on developing a set of measures paralleling the national income and product accounts.

At one level, this kind of effort can be subsumed under the general problem of data: research is dependent on the quantity, quality, comparability, and continuity of available data. Improvements in these characteristics can be obtained through a process of specifying data requirements, uncovering sources and institutionalizing data flows, and organizing the flows in response to user requirements. For urban problems, the relevant region would be the urban area, defined as the Standard Metropolitan Statistical Area (SMSA), or some similar area, such as a commuter field (where more than a specified fraction of resident workers commute to work places in the central city). Eventually, a consistent set of accounts applicable to all major metropolitan regions will be developed. As an example of work moving in this direction, estimates of personal income in individual metropolitan areas have recently been developed by the Department of Commerce.[8] But major data inadequacies remain, as attested to by most of the authors of the papers in *Issues in Urban Economics*.[9]

On another level, however, the regional accounts effort has evolved beyond the specification and organization of pertinent stock and flow variables into an attempt to answer the question, "Knowledge for what?" In one context, regional accounts that serve as an *information system* can furnish relevant information to public decision makers. In particular, such a system should reveal unpredicted consequences of actions that on the surface seem favorable or unobjectionable.[10] Again, regional accounts can yield a general system of relationships explaining economic activity in a region. In particular, public sector investment can be viewed as the key exogenous sector. An ultimate

8. This work is described in somewhat more detail in Appendix B, footnote 2.

9. For example, Stolnitz writes that a statistical blackout persists for the urban sector with respect to unemployment by occupation, industry, duration, and term of unemployment (*Issues*, p. 209); Margolis notes as a major data shortcoming the absence of measures of government product (*Issues*, p. 530); and Ornati points out that some data gaps stem from well-meaning, albeit misconstrued, rules forbidding collection of vital records by race or color (*Issues*, p. 338).

10. This approach is used by Werner Z. Hirsch and Sidney Sonenblum, "A Regional Information Design," Institute of Government and Public Affairs, University of California, Los Angeles, draft manuscript.

goal would be to develop such a system uniformly for all regions in the United States.[11]

Regional accounts must be much more than a disaggregation of the national income and product accounts. Additions suggested by Leven, Legler, and Shapiro include:[12]

1. Amounts and changes in capital stock and labor services;
2. Measures of the return to capital and labor, by industry for each region;
3. Components of per capita income and numbers of income recipients;
4. Changes in population beyond those in response to the filling of job vacancies;
5. Area characteristics affecting migration;
6. Regional exports (related to activity levels in other regions);
7. Public versus private capital stocks and changes in those stocks;
8. Receipts and expenditures of state and local government.

Because patterns of settlement and urban congestion seem part of the metropolitan development process, these measures are included:

9. Land use: production, institutional, government, and residential uses;
10. Land use intensity;
11. Measures of the spatial form of the region.

In retrospect, a feature of the material covered in this appendix is of considerable interest: though each subfield had its own set of concerns and focus, many interrelationships between the subfields emerged, confirming the usefulness of combining them into a general field of study.

---

11. This approach is used by Charles L. Leven, John B. Legler, and Perry Shapiro, "Designing a National System of Regional Accounts," unpublished manuscript revising working paper DRA 9, Washington University, 1968.

12. *Ibid.*

PART 2. THE STATE OF THE INSTITUTIONAL BASE

Appendix B
Evidence on Growth and Recognition of the Field

The discussion of institutional organization in the text of this report has focused on the state of university doctoral programs in the field and the efforts of CUE to promote development of the field. However, a much broader array of agencies and activities were involved in the field's development and/or now make up its institutional base. An attempt to document and appraise the field and its growth fully, covering all of the institutional base, would be a formidable task indeed and is beyond the scope of this report. Yet some developments in the field in this broad sense are worthy of note. Though the evidence marshaled is somewhat impressionistic, it does indicate substantial growth and corresponding recognition of urban economics as a distinct subfield of economics.

At the first meeting of CUE in October 1959, a number of organizations involved in urban economic research were identified. Some "significant ad hoc urban-regional studies" were listed, including studies in New York, St. Louis, and Pittsburgh, and the work of the Transportation Studies in Chicago and Philadelphia. The beginnings of urban economic research at universities were noted, and half-a-dozen centers identified. (A sample survey a few months later, however, documented rather low levels of activity.) Finally, the work of some research organizations was noted, including that of ACTION (American Council to Improve Our Neighborhoods), the Urban Land Institute, the National Bureau of Economic Research, and RFF itself.

Yet, it was concluded that, in 1959, there was "a dearth of economic research in urban affairs which would satisfy high standards of scholarship" and that "the field is very diffuse, and there is very little intellectual intercourse among people working in the field and its various allied efforts."[1] In the ten years since, there has been a marked increase in activities meeting high standards of scholarship. Those activities now seem part of a much more coherent and integrated whole.

A large number of agencies have embarked on urban economics research. There have been additional Transportation Studies, including a massive New

---

1. From Minutes of the first meeting of the Committee on Urban Economics, October 9, 1959.

York City effort. The RAND Corporation has carried out a series of studies of urban transportation. The establishment of cabinet departments of Health, Education, and Welfare; Housing and Urban Development; and Transportation involves a broadening of the federal research base in urban studies, including urban economics, while the recently organized Urban Institute forms another base of activity. There is a substantial amount of university research in urban economics, as documented in Appendix C.

Some current programs and developments furnish additional documentation. The RAND Corporation has organized a group to study urban problems in New York City; part of the effort, under the direction of Ira Lowry, involves the economics of housing in the city. The National Bureau of Economic Research has a newly formed group that is working on urban models under the direction of John Meyer and John Kain. The Institute of Public Administration has evaluated the rehabilitation of urban housing and estimated the costs involved (which generally turn out to be so high that they appear uneconomic). The organization of university instructors in real estate has recently inserted urban economics into its title, and is now the American Real Estate and Urban Economics Association.

The National Income Division of the Department of Commerce has developed new data series on personal income in metropolitan areas.[2] The Bureau of Labor Statistics of the Department of Labor has issued a new series on comparative living costs between metropolitan areas, in terms of "the city worker's family budget, moderate living standards." The series lists metropolitan area comparisons in dollar-value terms for the first time.[3]

Table B-1 exhibits the incidence of publication in four of the major journals of articles in urban economics.[4]

For the four major journals as a group, an increase over time occurred, but

---

2. R. E. Graham and E. J. Coleman, "Personal Income in Metropolitan Areas: A New Series," *Survey of Current Business* (May 1967); and Graham and Coleman, "Metropolitan Area Incomes, 1929-66," *Survey of Current Business* (August 1968). The series contains measures of total and per capita personal income for all of the SMSA's in the nation and covers seven years: 1929, 1940, 1950, 1959, 1962, 1965, and 1966. These are described as the first comprehensive measures for SMSA's. Work on the series was initiated on the basis of a 1959 meeting of Under Secretary of the Treasury Fred C. Scribner, Jr.; Congressman Thomas Curtis; representatives of the Internal Revenue Service and the Department of Commerce; and Werner Z. Hirsch, chairman, Committee on Regional Accounts (CORA). The meeting was the culmination of efforts by CORA to promote the development of metropolitan income statistics.

3. U. S. Department of Labor, News Release USDL-8474 (October 25, 1967), and Phyllis Groom, "A New City Worker's Family Budget," *Monthly Labor Review* (November 1967), pp. 1-8.

4. A review was made of the *Journal of Economic Abstracts* (*JEA*) to locate articles published in journals other than these four. The figures obtained are of limited use because *JEA* commenced publication in 1963. Further, an increasing number of sources have been referenced since *JEA*'s initial publication, so that an increase in articles may reflect better coverage, rather than increased production. But this argument, in turn, is limited because some of the additional sources are newly published journals. For whatever they are worth, then, these totals were obtained for articles published in other journals: 1963, six; 1964, nine; 1965, fourteen; 1966, twenty-eight; and 1967, twenty-six.

37

Table B-1. Number of Articles[a] in Urban Economics Appearing in Four Major Economic Journals from 1959 through 1967.

Year	American Economic Review[b] (AER)	Review of Economics and Statistics (RES)	Journal of Political Economy (JPE)	Southern Economic Journal (SEJ)	Total— four journals
1967	9	5	2	4	20
1966	3	1	1	3	8
1965	2	7	0	0	9
1964	0	4	1	1	6
1963	3	3	2	1	9
1962	3	3	0	2	8
1961	4	2	2	0	8
1960	0	1	1	0	2
1959	0	2	1	1	4

[a] Includes "notes, comments, and replies" as well as articles per se.

[b] Includes papers appearing annually in each May issue of *Papers and Proceedings*.

apparently by steps. Thus, there were around three articles per year in the 1959-60 period; eight per year between 1961 and 1966; and a large increase to twenty in 1967. Looking at individual journals, it appears there has been some upward trend for three of the four, though there are pronounced fluctuations on a year-to-year basis. If we aggregate the articles in the four journals by three-year intervals, a pronounced upward trend emerges: fourteen for 1959-61, twenty-three for 1962-64, and thirty-seven for 1965-67.

There is a mild dampening of this trend if we adjust for possible overall growth by dividing the number of urban economics articles by the total number of articles appearing in those journals. Values of this measure are .019 for 1959-61, .032 for 1962-64, and .042 for 1965-67.[5]

In any event, it might be argued that increased output involves both a quantitative and a qualitative dimension. To amplify, there has been an interest in housing and real estate, urban transportation, metropolitan labor markets, and local finance for a good many years. Increased activity in each of these areas will yield more professional literature, in quantitative terms. But the integration of these areas, and their interrelation under the general head of urban

---

5. The total number of articles was 728, 715, and 886 for the three periods, respectively. The category "articles" includes notes, comments, and replies, but does not include discussions in the *Papers and Proceedings* issue of the *American Economic Review*. Most of the increase in the last period is concentrated in 1967 for all four journals. Thus, the range for number of articles for 1959 through 1966 was eighty-three to 108 for *AER*, fifty to sixty-three for *RES*, fifty-one to sixty-one for *JPE*, and twenty-nine to forty-three for *SEJ*. In 1967, the numbers were 140 for *AER*, eighty-three for *RES*, ninety-one for *JPE*, and fifty-seven for *SEJ*, a substantial increase in every case. This suggests a substantial growth in work in the field of economics, perhaps explicitly recognized by the journal editors. The large increase in 1967 to twenty articles in urban economics would, in part, be explained by the general increase in the total number of articles published.

Table B-2. Number of Economists by Subfield[a] and Specialty (1966)

Subfield and specialty, including specialty code number	Economists in subfield or specialty (primary area)	Number having doctorate
General economic theory	1,266	666
Economic history, History of thought	301	199
Economic systems, development, planning	931	499
Economic statistics	447	212
Monetary and fiscal theory and institutions	1,152	698
(State and local finance—9405)	(135)	(91)
International economics	633	327
Business finance and administration, marketing, and accounting	4,861	1,171
Industrial organizations, government and business, industry studies	764	375
(Public utilities, transportation, and service industries—9703)	(218)	(110)
Land economics	474	232
(Natural resources—9803)	(232)	(108)
Agricultural economics	1,204	657
Labor economics	767	410
Population; Welfare programs; Standards of living	185	91
(Public housing—9903)	(12)	(3)
Economics—Other	165	56
Total	13,150	5,593

a Subfields in parentheses.

Source: Letter from J. J. Brown, Associate Study Director, National Register Group, Office of Economics and Manpower Studies, National Science Foundation. Some of the data appear in the *National Register of Scientific and Technical Personnel, 1966.*

economics, is a qualitative change not susceptible to simple enumeration.

A final set of growth indicators is afforded by classification schemes of the National Science Foundation and the American Economic Association.

Every two years, the National Science Foundation carries out an enumeration of scientists for its *National Register of Scientific and Technical Personnel.* Urban economics as a specialty appeared for the first time in 1968. (A specialty is a component of a subfield.) In particular, these related specialties appeared:

16576 Urban economics and public policy
16584 Urban transportation economics
16626 Housing economics

Specialties are defined[6] on the basis of a dialogue between the National Science Foundation, government agencies, and an American Economic Associ-

6. Based on a conversation with J. J. Brown, Associate Study Director, National Register Group, Office of Economic and Manpower Studies, National Science Foundation, April 1968.

000 General economics; Theory; History; Systems
010 General economics
   011 General economics
020 General economic theory
   021 General equilibrium theory
   022 Microeconomic theory
   023 Macroeconomic theory
   024 Welfare theory
030 History of thought; methodology
   031 History of economic thought
   032 Economic methodology
040 Economic history
   041 Economic history
050 Economic systems
   051 Capitalist economic systems
   052 Socialist and communist economic systems
   053 Comparative economic systems
090 Other
   099 Other (specify)

100 Economic growth; Development; Planning; Fluctuations
110 Economic growth, development, and planning theory and policy
   111 Economic growth and development theory
   112 Economic planning theory and policy
   113 Economics of war and defense
120 Economic development studies
   121 Economic development studies of less developed countries
   122 Economic development studies of developed countries
   123 Comparative economic development studies
130 Economic fluctuations and forecasting
   131 Economic fluctuations and stabilization
   132 Economic forecasting and forecasting models
190 Other
   199 Other (specify)

200 Economic statistics
210 Econometric and statistical methods
   211 Econometric methods
   212 Statistical methods
220 Economic and social accounting
   221 National income accounting
   222 Input-output
   223 Financial accounts
   224 National wealth and balance sheets
   225 Social indicators and accounts
290 Other
   299 Other (specify)

300 Monetary and fiscal theory and institutions
310 Monetary and financial theory and institutions
   311 Monetary theory and policy
   312 Commercial banking
   313 Financial markets
   314 Financial intermediaries
320 Fiscal policy and public finance
   321 Fiscal theory and policy
   322 Government expenditures and budgeting
   323 Taxation
   324 State and local finance
390 Other
   399 Other (specify)

400 International economics
410 International trade theory
   411 International trade theory
420 Trade relations; commercial policy; economic integration
   421 Trade relations
   422 Commercial policy
   423 Economic integration
430 Balance of payments; international finance
   431 Balance of payments; exchange rates
   432 International monetary arrangements
440 International investment and foreign aid
   441 International investment and foreign aid
490 Other
   499 Other (specify)

500 Administration; Business finance; Marketing; Accounting
510 Administration
   511 Organization and decision theory
   512 Managerial economics
   513 Business and public administration
520 Business finance and investment
   521 Business finance
   522 Business investment
530 Insurance
   531 Insurance
540 Marketing
   541 Marketing
550 Accounting
   551 Accounting
590 Other
   599 Other (specify)

600 Industrial organization; Technological change; Industry studies
610 Industrial organization and public policy
   611 Industrial organization and market structure
   612 Public policy towards monopoly and competition
   613 Public utilities and government regulation of the private sector
   614 Public enterprises
   615 Economics of transportation
620 Economics of technological change
   621 Technological change; innovation; research and development
630 Industry studies
   631 Industry studies: manufacturing
   632 Industry studies: extractive industries
   633 Industry studies: distributive trades
   634 Industry studies: construction
   635 Industry studies: services and other
690 Other
   699 Other (specify)

700 Agriculture; Natural resources
710 Agriculture
   711 Agricultural demand and supply analysis
   712 Agricultural situation and outlook
   713 Agricultural policy
   714 Agricultural finance
   715 Agricultural marketing
   716 Farm management
   717 Land reform
720 Natural resources
   721 Natural resources and conservation
790 Other
   799 Other (specify)

800 Manpower; Labor; Population
810 Manpower training and development
   811 Manpower training and development
820 Labor markets; public policy
   821 Theory of labor markets
   822 Public policy; role of government
   823 Labor mobility; migration
   824 Labor market studies, wages, employment
830 Trade unions; collective bargaining; labor-management relations
   831 Trade unions; collective bargaining; labor-management relations
840 Population
   841 Population
890 Other
   899 Other (specify)

900 Welfare programs; Consumer economics; Urban and regional economics
910 Welfare programs
   911 General welfare programs
   912 Economics of education
   913 Economics of health
   914 Economics of poverty
   915 Social security
920 Consumer economics
   921 Consumer economics; levels and standards of living
➤ 930 Urban economics
   931 Urban economics and public policy
   932 Housing economics
   933 Urban transportation economics
940 Regional economics
   941 Regional economics
990 Other
   999 Other (specify)

Source: Report of the Committee on Classification, Richard H. Leftwich, chairman, *American Economic Review* (May 1968), pp. 711-22. Reproduced with permission of the American Economic Association.

ation committee representing all the professional economic organizations.

The statistical results of the 1968 survey will not be available until late 1969. Presumably, summary information will then appear on numbers of economists listing these specialties as primary fields or as one of four secondary fields; and on the distribution of degree attainment, salary, and type of employment, by specialty.

In lieu of that more pertinent information, Table B-2 lists subfield and specialty information, as of 1966. Some of the specialties are related fairly closely to urban economics.

The American Economic Association is in the process of revising its classification scheme for economics as a discipline. It has been recommended that a single system of classification should be developed for all indexing and classification activities of the association.[7] This would serve (1) the listing of current economic literature, (2) the cumulative indexing of economic literature, and (3) the listing of economic specialties for the *American Economics Association Handbook* and the *National Register of Scientific and Technical Personnel*.

The three-level scheme reproduced opposite has been formulated; variations of this will yield the specialty list and the current literature classification. In it, urban economics and related fields appear as specialties, and are indicated by arrow. A fourth level of detail for cumulative indexing is still under review, and will be based on experience with the new system.

Clearly, the revised listing of current literature will be much more useful than the present scheme, in which urban economics is an implicit component of "Land Economics; Agricultural Economics; Economic Geography; Housing." In sum, it seems clear that urban economics has received general recognition as a well-defined area of specialization.

---

7. Richard H. Leftwich, "Report of the Committee on Classification," *American Economic Review* (May 1968), pp. 711-22.

Appendix C
Urban Economics Programs for the Doctorate

In its review of the state of the field, this report is primarily concerned with doctoral programs in urban economics as offered by universities in the United States. Information on the availability and major features of such programs was secured by a questionnaire sent during 1968 to 149 departments (ninety-eight economics departments and fifty-one business schools) that offered the doctorate in economics or business administration.[1] Initial response to the questionnaire was good and several follow-up requests helped bring the total number of replies to 145, a 97 per cent rate of response. Hence, essentially the entire population was surveyed.

The departments contacted and a classification of replies received appear in Table C-1. Apart from the few departments that did not respond, the table's basic classification is that of existence versus nonexistence of a program in urban economics. (A further breakdown covers some cases of interest; for example, the existence of an interdisciplinary doctorate.)

Most cases were straightforward, but in the occasional marginal cases for which classification took some thought, the university decision was generally followed. For example, some departments with a field in regional economics felt that their program contained enough urban economics to fall within the definition of urban economics as a field; others felt that their program did not fit the definition. The departmental decision was accepted in these cases. Other marginal cases, and classifications adopted, are indicated in the table.

The information in Table C-1 has been summarized in Table C-2, which shows the number of doctoral programs in urban economics that were available in 1968 or planned for 1969. Forty economics departments and thirteen business schools offered or were initiating the field for the doctorate; respectively, these comprise roughly 40 per cent of the economics departments and

---

1. The term "department" refers to both economics departments and business schools; the latter, in turn, covers graduate schools of business administration, colleges of business, etc. Sources drawn on in compiling the list of departments included: June Graham, ed., *A Guide to Graduate Study*, 3rd ed. (American Council on Education, 1965); Allan M. Cartter, ed., *American Universities and Colleges*, 9th ed. (American Council on Education, 1964); and E. R. Wasserman and E. E. Switzer, *The Random House Guide to Graduate Study in the Arts and Sciences* (Random House, 1967). Lists of departmental chairmen were obtained for economics departments from the American Economic Association and for schools of business from the *Directory of Members, Officers, Committees 1967-68* (American Association of Collegiate Schools of Business, 1968). The final formulation of the list of business schools to be contacted drew on the informed judgment of Arthur Weimer.

42

Table C-1. Classification of Replies to the Survey Questionnaire on Doctoral Programs in Urban Economics (1968)

* = Urban economics program in existence.

*C = CUE-supported program.

*I = Program with interdisciplinary doctorate.

*R = Program in regional economics including training in urban economics.

*N = New program to be introduced.

—— = Joint program.

*——(*) = Collaborative program, with major program features in department shown without parentheses.

No = No program.

X = No reply.

I = Interdisciplinary doctorate but not enough urban economics to classify as program.

R = Program in regional economics with little training in urban economics.

RS = Regional science program.

A blank indicates that a department was not contacted. This was because there was no department in the given discipline; the department did not offer the doctorate; or, in the case of some business schools, outside information indicated absence of the field.

State	University	Economics department	Business school	State	University	Economics department	Business school
Ala.	U. of Alabama	No		Fla.	Florida State U.	*R	No
Ariz.	U. of Arizona	No			U. of Florida	*N	*
Ark.	U. of Arkansas	No	No	Ga.	Georgia State		
Calif.	Stanford U.	*N	No		College	X	X
	U. of California,				U. of Georgia	No	No
	Berkeley	No	*	Ill.	Illinois Institute		
	U. of California,				of Technology	No	
	Los Angeles	*C	*		Northwestern U.	No	No
	U. of California,				S. Ill. U.	No	
	Riverside	No			U. of Illinois,		
	U. of California,				Urbana	*	*
	Davis	No			U. of Chicago	*C	——(*)
	U. of California,			Ind.	Indiana U.	(*)	——*C
	Santa Barbara	No			Purdue U.		No
	Claremont				Notre Dame U.	No	No
	Colleges	No		Iowa	Iowa State U.	*C	
	U. of Southern				U. of Iowa	*	
	California	*	*	Kan.	Kansas State U.	No	
Colo.	U. of Colorado	*N	No		U. of Kansas	No	No
	Colorado State U.	No		Ky.	U. of Kentucky	*R	No
Conn.	U. of Connecticut	No		La.	Louisiana State U.		No
	Yale U.	No			Tulane U.	No	
D. C.	American U.	No	*	Md.	Johns Hopkins U.	*	
	Georgetown U.	*			U. of Maryland	*R	No
	George Washington			Mass.	Clark U.	No	
	University	No	No		Tufts U.	No	
	Catholic U.	No			Harvard U.	*	I

Table C-1. *Continued*

State	University	Economics department	Business school	State	University	Economics department	Business school
Mass. (cont.)	Mass. Inst. of Technology	*	No	Ohio	U. of Cincinnati	R	No
	U. of Mass.	No	No		Ohio State U.	No	No
	Boston College	No			Case-Western Reserve U.	*	
	Boston U.	*N		Okla.	Oklahoma State U.	No	
Mich.	U. of Michigan	*N	*I		U. of Oklahoma	*N	
	Michigan State U.	No	No	Oreg.	U. of Oregon	R	No
	Wayne State U.	*C		Pa.	Penn State U.	No	No
Minn.	U. of Minnesota	No	X		Bryn Mawr College	No	
Miss.	Mississippi State U.	No			U. of Pittsburgh	*C	No
	U. of Mississippi	No			U. of Pa.	No	RS
Mo.	St. Louis U.	*N[a]	No		Lehigh U.	No	
	U. of Missouri	*R	No		Carnegie-Mellon U.	*	X
	Washington U., St. Louis	*C	No	R. I.	Brown U.	*C	
Nebr.	U. of Nebraska	No	No		U. of Rhode Island	No	
N. C.	U. of N. C.	No	No	Tenn.	Vanderbilt U.	No	
	Duke U.	*N			U. of Tennessee	*N ——*N	
N. J.	Princeton U.	*		Texas	Rice U.	No	
	Rutgers U.	No			U. of Houston	No	
N. Mex.	U. of New Mexico	No			Southern Methodist U.	*	
N. Y.	Fordham U.	No			U. of Texas	No	No
	New School for Social Research	No			Texas A. & M. U.	*	
	Cornell U.	No	No	S. Dak.	South Dakota State U.	No	
	New York U.	*C, I——(*)[b]		Utah	U. of Utah	*N	
	Columbia U.	*	No	Va.	U. of Virginia	No	No
	Syracuse U.	*C, I	No	Wash.	U. of Washington, Seattle	*I	*
	State University of New York, Buffalo	No	No		Washington State U.	No	
	U. of Rochester	No	No	W. Va.	U. of West Virginia	*	
	City University of New York	*		Wis.	U. of Wisconsin, Madison	No	*
	Rensselaer Polytechnic Institute	No					

[a] Classified under economics for ease of exposition. St. Louis University has a Department of Urban Affairs in which several persons from economics will present courses.

[b] Classified under economics for ease of exposition. Most courses in urban economics at New York University are offered by the Graduate School of Public Administration, although instructors are economists and the economics department uses those courses in an urban economics program for the Ph.D. The CUE grant was made to the Graduate School of Public Administration and the Graduate School of Business Administration.

20 per cent of the business schools replying to the questionnaire. The total of fifty-three departments offering the field comprises 35 per cent of the 145 which replied. In addition, nine other departments expressed interest in introducing the field in the future.

As an item of incidental interest, Cartter's classification of economics departments by quality of graduate faculty[2] was used to relate the availability of a program in the field to the quality of graduate education in economics. (This classification was highly correlated with a similar classification of quality of graduate education in Cartter's report; the former was used because it was

Table C-2. Summary of Responses on Availability of Doctoral Programs in Urban Economics (1968)

	Economics departments	Business schools	All
Departments with programs			
CUE-supported	9[a]	1	10
Other departments			
Urban economics program	16[b]	10[c]	26
Interdisciplinary doctorate	1	1	2
Regional-urban program	4	0	4
New program being initiated	10[d]	1	11
Total	40	13	53
Departments with no programs[e]	57[f]	35[g]	92
No response to questionnaire	1	3	4
Grand total	98	51	149

[a] Includes New York University, where most courses in urban economics are given in public administration (see Table C-1, footnote b). Also includes Syracuse University, which offers an interdisciplinary doctorate, as well as the doctorate in economics.

[b] Includes Indiana University economics department, but program is centered in the business school.

[c] Includes the University of Chicago and New York University business schools, with programs respectively centered in the economics department and the Graduate School of Business Administration.

[d] Includes St. Louis University, where urban economics courses are given in the urban affairs department (see Table C-1, footnote a).

[e] Of these departments, nine expressed an interest in a later introduction of an urban economics program. Of these, eight are economics departments and one is a business school. The economics departments are at the University of California, Riverside; American University; Clark University; Boston College; the University of Minnesota; Fordham University; Bryn Mawr College; and the University of Rhode Island. The business school is at Northwestern University.

[f] Includes the University of Cincinnati and the University of Oregon; both have doctoral programs in regional economics but not enough urban economics to classify as a program.

[g] Includes Harvard University, which offers an urban studies program, and the University of Pennsylvania, which offers a program in regional science.

more detailed.) Cartter classified departments rated above average in quality into four groups: distinguished, strong, good, and adequate plus. Thirty-six departments fell within one of these four categories. Thirty-five departments of lower quality, classified under the headings of marginal or not sufficient, were not explicitly identified. Thus, Cartter's report covered seventy-one economics departments, compared to the ninety-eight surveyed in the present report. (It seems a reasonable guess that the twenty-seven departments excluded from the Cartter report but appearing in the present survey would tend to be classified in the lower categories, if only because such an exclusion itself involves an evaluation.)

When the departments in each category were enumerated in terms of whether or not they had a program in urban economics, it turned out that urban economics was much more prevalent in the highly ranked (rated adequate plus or better) departments of economics. (See Table C-3.) Programs were offered by more than half of the highly ranked departments but by less than one-third of the other departments. The difference is statistically significant.[3] Thus, it would appear that the more prestigious departments have been more innovative, in terms of propensity to introduce the new field of urban economics.

Within the highly ranked departments, there is some appearance of difference between classes, because the highest and lowest groups have a greater propensity to offer the field than the two middle groups. This difference, however, was not statistically significant.[4]

The very recent development of urban economics as a field is indicated in Table C-4, which shows the year during which a doctoral program in the field was established by all economics departments that have programs. The following items seem noteworthy:

- There is an accelerating trend in the introduction of the field.
- Roughly half of the departments introduced the field in 1967 or later; 1967 was the median date of introduction of the field.
- For departments supported by CUE matching grants, the median date of introduction of the field is 1963. (For those receiving major grants, the median date is 1961; for those receiving pilot grants, the median date is 1964.) Not surprisingly, the CUE-supported departments were pioneers in the field; they were members of the relatively small set of departments that offered the field at the time the matching grant program was established.

---

2. Allan M. Cartter, *An Assessment of Quality in Graduate Education* (American Council on Education, 1966), pp. 34-38. The ratings were made by samples of department chairmen, senior scholars, and junior scholars in economics. Results used here are for the combined samples.

3. The cross-classification of high quality-other and program-no-program can be viewed as a contingency table. In this formulation a χ^2 statistic can be used to test the hypothesis of independence of the basic characteristics. The calculated χ^2 obtained was 7.21; the tabled χ^2 at the 95th percentile is 3.84 (for one degree of freedom). Hence the null hypothesis is rejected.

4. The calculated χ^2 was 1.79 as opposed to a tabled χ^2 of 7.81 at the 95th percentile for three degrees of freedom.

Table C-3. Availability of Field of Urban Economics Related to Quality of Faculty for Economics Departments

Quality of graduate faculty by department	Program in field[a]	No program in field	Quality of graduate faculty by department	Program in field[a]	No program in field
Distinguished[b]			Good (cont.)		
Massachusetts Inst. of Technology	X		U. of Illinois	X	
Harvard U.	X		Indiana U.	X	
Yale U.		X	Iowa State U.	X	
Stanford U.	X		Michigan State U.		X
U. of California, Berkeley		X	U. of North Carolina		X
Princeton U.	X		Purdue U.		X
U. of Chicago	X		U. of Rochester		X
	—	—	Vanderbilt U.		X
Subtotal	5	2	U. of Virginia		X
			U. of Washington, Seattle	X	
Strong[b]			Subtotal	6	7
U. of Wisconsin		X			
U. of Michigan	X				
Northwestern U.		X	Adequate plus[e]		
Carnegie Mellon U.	X		Claremont Colleges		X
Johns Hopkins U.	X		U. of Maryland	X	
U. of Minnesota		X	New York U.	X	
Columbia U.	X		U. of Pittsburgh	X	
U. of Pennsylvania		X	Syracuse U.	X	
U. of California, Los Angeles	X		U. of Texas		X
	—	—	Washington U., St. Louis	X	
Subtotal	5	4	Subtotal	5	2
Good[c]					
Brown U.	X		Total highly rated	21	15
Cornell U.		X	All other departments[d]	19	43[e]
Duke U.	X		Grand total	40	58

a Includes departments that offered the field in 1968 and those introducing the field in 1969.

b Departments are listed in order of ranking.

c Departments are listed alphabetically.

d The Cartter survey of rated departments included seventy-one departments of economics; thirty-six were rated above average in quality and thirty-five below average. Hence, the sixty-two departments here include thirty-five rated below average, and twenty-seven not covered by Cartter.

e Includes one case of non-response to the questionnaire of this report.

Sources: Allan M. Cartter, An Assessment of Quality in Graduate Education (American Council on Education, 1966), pp. 34-38, and questionnaire responses.

Table C-4. Date of Establishment of Doctoral Programs in Urban Economics by Economics Departments

Year	Economics departments CUE-supported	All other	Total
1969	0	9[a]	9
1968	1	6[a]	7
1967	0	5	5
1966	1	4	5
1965	1[b]	1	2
1964	1	3	4
1963	2	0	2
1962	1	0	1
1961	2	1	3
1960	0	1	1
1959	1	0	1
Total	10	30	40

[a] In its response to the 1968 questionnaire, one department interpreted "introducing next year" to mean that the program would be introduced in 1968, presumably referring to the academic year.

[b] Refers to Indiana University; the program is centered in the business school. In general, business schools were not included because they listed dates that often applied to the establishment of real estate, rather than urban economics, programs.

Responses to other questionnaire items have been tabulated and are presented at this point for forty-four departments offering the field. This group includes thirty-eight university departments with programs in effect in 1968[5] and six of the eleven introducing the field in 1969. Those six filled out the questionnaire to at least some extent.

The continued growth of the field of urban economics is indicated by an apparently large demand for faculty by the departments responding. Thus, twenty-six departments planned to expand their faculty in 1969, as opposed to eleven that did not plan expansion and seven that were unsure or did not respond.

In fourteen of the forty-four cases, there was an interdisciplinary program in urban studies that led to the doctorate. (But this occurred for only one of the ten CUE-supported departments.)

Research centers or institutes are popular; thirty-four of the forty-four

5. Four of the forty-two departments that offered the field in 1968 are excluded for the following reasons. At Indiana University, the economics department is excluded because its collaborative program is centered in the business school; at the University of Chicago, the business school is excluded because its collaborative program is centered in the economics department. Similarly, the business school at New York University was involved in a collaborative program with the Graduate School of Public Administration and the economics department. The program is administered by economists housed in public administration but is classified under economics for ease of exposition. The business school at the University of Illinois is excluded because of a very limited response on its questionnaire.

departments reported that such an organization existed on their campus. (The Massachusetts Institute of Technology listed two.) In about half the cases, these organizations were established at about the time that the field was introduced, while in about one-third of the cases, the center was established before, and in one-sixth of the cases, after the introduction of the field (see Table C-5).

Table C-5. Relation Between Date of Establishment of Research Center or Institute and Introduction of Field

When research center was established relative to introduction of field	Number of cases
More than a year before	9[a]
Within a year before	3
Same year	10[a]
Within a year after	5
More than a year after	5
Information not available	3
	—
Total	35

[a] The Massachusetts Institute of Technology listed two institutes.

Faculty in Urban Economics

In terms of full-time equivalent (FTE) man-years, roughly 100 man-years of faculty time per year were devoted to urban economics in the forty-four departments. One hundred and eighty-six persons were engaged in the field. Detailed information on faculty appears in Tables C-6, C-7, and C-8. Table C-6 lists total faculty time by departmental categories. It shows that CUE-supported departments accounted for about one-quarter both of FTE and of the number of persons involved. About 70 per cent of total faculty were in economics departments; the remaining 30 per cent were in business schools. The amount of time spent on teaching and on research were roughly equal. About half of the individuals involved devoted half or more of their teaching time to urban economics. (Teaching time as a fraction of total time will, of course, vary between individuals.)

Table C-7 lists faculty averages by departmental category in terms of FTE and of individuals. In all categories, there was roughly equal distribution of faculty time between research and teaching. In CUE-supported departments, the average FTE was larger than that of all other departments; similarly, business schools had a larger FTE than economics departments.

Table C-8 lists faculty FTE and number of persons by individual departments, for all departments with a field in urban economics. One of the problems underlying these comparisons is the question of the kind of courses and research to be classified as urban economics. In developing the results presented here, departmental self-classifications were accepted. This leads to a broad definition of the field, and to some lack of comparability in a few cases.

Table C-6. Faculty in Forty-four Urban Economics Programs: Full-Time Equivalent (Man-Years) and Number of Individuals Involved—Summary Statistics (1968)

Groupings of departments	Full-time equivalent (man-years)			Number of individuals involved			
	Teaching time	Research time	Total (1) + (2)	Those with half or more of teaching load in field	Other instructors in field[a]	Faculty not teaching but engaged in research in field	Total (4) + (5) + (6)
	(1)	(2)	(3)	(4)	(5)	(6)	(7)
CUE-supported departments	15.08	14.28	29.36	29	15	8	52
Departments initiating new program	3.85	3.40	7.25	6	6	1	13
All other departments	31.61	40.05	71.66	54	27	40	121
Total	50.54	57.73	108.27	89	48	49	186
Economics departments[b]	34.04	41.98	76.02	64	31	41	136
Business schools[c]	16.50	15.75	32.25	25	17	8	50
Total	50.54	57.73	108.27	89	48	49	186

[a] Includes non-economists and teaching assistants; i.e., those not on regular faculty.
[b] Includes one Department of Urban Affairs (University of Missouri).
[c] Includes one joint program: economics and business administration (University of Tennessee).

Table C-7. Faculty in Forty-four Urban Economics Programs: Average per Department (1968)

Department	Full-time equivalent (man-years)			Number of individuals involved			
	Teaching time	Research time	Total (1) + (2)	Those with half or more of teaching load in the field	Other instructors in field	Faculty not teaching but engaged in research in field	Total (4) + (5) + (6)
	(1)	(2)	(3)	(4)	(5)	(6)	(7)
CUE-supported departments (10 cases)	1.51	1.43	2.94	2.9	1.5	0.8	5.2
Departments initiating new program (6 cases)	0.64	0.57	1.21	1.0	1.0	0.2	2.2
All other departments (28 cases)	1.13	1.43	2.56	1.9	1.0	1.4	4.3
Departments with programs in effect							
Economics departments (29 cases)	1.04	1.32	2.36	2.0	0.9	1.3	4.2
Business schools (9 cases)	1.75	1.67	3.42	2.6	1.9	0.8	5.3

Table C-8. Faculty in Urban Economics Programs: Full-Time Equivalent (Man-Years) and Individuals Involved, By Department (1968)

Department (E = Economics department, B = Business school)	Full-time equivalent (man-years)			Number of individuals involved			
	Teaching time	Research time	Total (1) + (2)	With half or more of teaching load in the field	Other instructors in the field[a]	Faculty not teaching but engaged in research in field	Total (4) + (5) + (6)
	(1)	(2)	(3)	(4)	(5)	(6)	(7)
CUE-supported departments: recipients of CUE matching grants							
U. of California, Los Angeles (E)	1.75	2.25	4.00	3	1	2	6
Indiana U. (B)	1.50	1.00	2.50	2	0	1	3
Wayne State U. (E)	2.00	1.50	3.50	4	1	0	5
Washington U. (E)	1.50	2.00	3.50	5	1	0	6
Syracuse U. (E)	2.33	1.33	3.66	5	2	1	8
U. of Chicago (E)	1.00	1.00	2.00	1	4	1	6
Iowa State U. (E)	1.00	1.75	2.75	2	1	1	4
New York U. (E)	1.50	2.00	3.50	4	1	2	7
U. of Pittsburgh (E)	2.00	1.20	3.20	2	3	0	5
Brown U. (E)	0.50	0.25	0.75	1	1	0	2
Departments initiating new programs							
Stanford U. (E)	1.00	1.00	2.00	2	0	0	2
U. of Colorado (E)	0.10	0.15	0.25	0	3	0	3
U. of Florida (E)	1.00	0.50	1.50	2	1	0	3
St. Louis U. (Urban Affairs)	0.50	0.50	1.00	1	0	0	1
Duke U. (E)	0.50	0.50	1.00	0	2	0	2
U. of Tennessee (Joint: Finance-Economics)	0.75	0.75	1.50	1	0	1	2
All other departments							
U. of California, Berkeley (B)	3.00	2.00	5.00	3	3	1	7

Institution						
U. of California, Los Angeles (B)[b]	3.00	6.00	6	0	0	6
U. of Southern California (E)	0.50	1.00	1	0	0	1
U. of Southern California (B)	1.00	2.00	3	2	3	8
American U. (B)	2.50	3.00	2	7	0	9
Georgetown U. (E)[b]	0.33	0.33	0	1	0	1
Florida State U. (E)	1.00	3.00	3	0	0	3
U. of Florida (B)	3.50	5.00	2	4	0	6
U. of Illinois, Urbana (E)	0.67	1.17	1	0	4	5
U. of Iowa (E)	2.00	4.00	2	2	0	4
U. of Kentucky (E)	2.00	3.50	2	0	2	4
Johns Hopkins U. (E)	0.33	0.66	1	0	0	1
U. of Maryland (E)	2.00	2.50	2	0	1	3
Harvard U. (E)[c]	1.25	2.00	2	2	0	4
Massachusetts Institute of Technology (E)	2.00	3.25	1	3	7	11
U. of Michigan (B)[b]	0.25	1.00	1	1	0	2
U. of Missouri (E)	3.00	4.50	4	0	4	8
Princeton U. (E)	1.00	2.00	1	0	3	4
Columbia U. (E)	1.00	2.25	2	1	2	5
City U. of New York (E)	3.00	4.00	3	1	6	10
Case-Western Reserve U. (E)[b]	0.50	1.00	1	0	0	1
Carnegie-Mellon U. (E)	0.20[d]	2.00	1	0	2	3
Southern Methodist U. (E)	0.75	0.75	0	0	2	2
Texas A&M U. (E)	0.25	2.00	1	0	1	2
U. of Washington (E)[b]	0.50	0.50	1	0	0	1
U. of Washington (B)	1.75	5.00	3	0	2	5
West Virginia U. (E)	1.50	3.00	3	0	0	3
U. of Wisconsin (B)	0.75	1.25	2	0	0	2

[a] Includes non-economists and teaching assistants, i.e., non-regular faculty.

[b] Teaching-research man-years not given on questionnaire, so estimated from other information given.

[c] Questionnaire response advised that urban economics research time cannot be extricated from regional economics. Research time estimated by multiplying teaching time by 1.6, the factor that holds for the Massachusetts Institute of Technology.

[d] Estimate based on response indicating seminars but no formal courses in field.

However, inspection of course offerings and research topics indicated that this problem was not a major source of difficulty.

Course Work and Enrollment in Courses

Departments now offering programs in urban economics list 163 courses in the field, of which 132 carry graduate credit. CUE-supported departments offer sixty-two courses—38 per cent of the total. There were approximately thirty-five hundred course enrollments per year for all courses in the field; enrollments in CUE-supported departments made up a third of the total. Course enrollments are on an annual basis over the years 1967 and 1968. Undergraduate enrollment per course averaged thirty-seven and graduate enrollment averaged eighteen.[6] Six departments introducing the field in 1969 listed thirteen courses with catalog approval.

Table C-9 lists summary data and Table C-10 lists detailed data on number of and enrollment in courses existing in 1968. Table C-11 lists the distribution of dates of approval of courses for existing and future programs. The very recent development of the field is again illustrated by the preponderance of approval dates within the last five years.

Table C-9. Number of Courses and Annual Total Enrollment in Courses in Urban Economics—Summary Statistics

Department	Number of courses (1968)			Students enrolled in courses on annual basis (average 1967-68)		
	Under-graduate credit only	Graduate credit	Total	Under-graduate credit only	Graduate credit	Total
CUE-supported departments	9	53	62	260	940	1,200
All other departments	22	79	101	885	1,419	2,304
Total	31	132	163	1,145	2,359	3,504

Postdoctoral Fellows, Persons Awarded Doctorates, and Precandidacy Students

Information on numbers of postdoctoral fellows, persons awarded doctorates, and precandidacy students appears in Table C-12. Postdoctoral fellowships are essentially an institutional feature of the CUE matching grant program; twenty of the twenty-one cases are located at CUE-supported departments.

Seventy doctorates were listed as completed in the last five years and ninety were under way. The CUE-supported department share in these categories is substantial, being more than half of the total in each case. It should be noted, however, that there is likely to be some understatement of total doctorates

---

6. In several cases, enrollment was not given on questionnaire responses, so a "reasonable" estimate was employed. See Table C-10, footnote b, for specifics.

Table C-10. Number of Courses and Annual Total Enrollment in Courses in Urban Economics—Detail

Department (E = Economics department, B = Business school)	Number of courses (1968)			Students enrolled in courses on annual basis (average 1967-68)		
	Undergraduate credit only	Graduate credit	Total	Undergraduate credit only	Graduate credit	Total
CUE-supported departments						
U. of California, Los Angeles (E)	3	4	7	80	50	130
Indiana U. (B)	1	5	6	40	120	160
Wayne State U. (E)	0	5	5	0	100	100
Washington U. (E)	0	6	6	0	60	60
Syracuse U. (E)	2	6	8	65	195	260
U. of Chicago (E)	0	6	6	0	125	125
Iowa State U. (E)	2	6	8	40	25	65
New York U. (E)	1	6	7	35	125	160
Pittsburgh U. (E)	0	6	6	0	125	125
Brown U. (E)	0	3	3	0	15	15
All other departments						
U. of California, Berkeley (B)	4	2	6	180	88	268
U. of California, Los Angeles (B)[a]	3	8	11	180	120	300
U. of Southern California (E)	0	2	2	0	25	25
U. of Southern California (B)	0	3	3	0	58	58
American U. (B)	0	8	8	0	306	306
Georgetown U. (E)	1	1	2	25[b]	10[b]	35[b]
Florida State U. (E)	3	5	8	75[b]	50[b]	125[b]
U. of Florida (B)	2	6	8	58	28	86
U. of Illinois, Urbana (E)	0	3	3	0	60	60
U. of Iowa (E)	2	3	5	21	35	56
U. of Kentucky (E)	0	4	4	0	70	70

Table C-10. (Continued)

Department (E = Economics department B = Business school)	Number of courses (1968)			Students enrolled in courses on annual basis (average 1967-68)		
	Under- graduate credit only	Grad- uate credit	Total	Under- graduate credit only	Grad- uate credit	Total
Johns Hopkins U. (E)	0	1	1	0	25	25
U. of Maryland (E)	0	3	3	0	30[b]	30[b]
Harvard U. (E)	1	1	2	49	9	58
Massachusetts Institute of Technology (E)	2	3	5	14	52	66
U. of Michigan (B)	0	2	2	0	56	56
U. of Missouri (E)	0	2	2	0	13	13
Princeton U. (E)	1	1	2	30	20	50
Columbia U. (E)	0	3	3	0	60	60
City U. of New York (E)	0	3	3	0	85	85
Case-Western Reserve U. (E)	1	2	3	25[b]	20[b]	45[b]
Carnegie-Mellon U. (E)[c]	0	0	0	0	0	0
Southern Methodist U. (E)	0	0	0	0	0	0
Texas A&M U. (E)	0	1	1	0	10[b]	10[b]
U. of Washington (E)	0	2	2	0	40	40
U. of Washington (B)	2	2	4	228	52	280
West Virginia U. (E)	0	3	3	0	40	40
U. of Wisconsin (B)	0	5	5	0	57	57

[a] Estimate based on some given data.

[b] Enrollment per undergraduate course estimated as 25; graduate course estimated as 10.

[c] Department has seminars but no formal course in the field. No data on seminar enrollment given.

Table C-11. Distribution of Dates of Approval of Courses for Catalog

Date course approved	Number of courses			
	CUE-supported departments (10 cases)	All other departments (28 cases)	Six departments initiating new program	All depart-ments
1968 or later	0	14	5	19
1967	7	18	1	26
1966	18	13	1	32
1965	4	8	0	12
1964	5	8	1	14
1963	3	2	0	5
1962	5	1	0	6
1961	1	4	0	5
1960	1	4	0	5
1959	2	2	0	4
Pre-1959	1	5	2	8
No date listed	15	22	3	40
Total	62	101	13	176

Table C-12. Data on Postdoctoral Fellows, Persons Awarded Doctorates, and Precandidacy Students (1968)

Category	Number of cases[a]		
	CUE-supported departments	All other departments	Total
Postdoctoral fellows (1966-68)	20	1	21
Persons awarded doctorates (1963-68)	38	32	70
Doctoral candidates	52	38[b]	90
Precandidacy students			
Economics	80	94+	174
Business schools	14	26+	40
All other	29	45+	74
Total[c]	123	165+	288

[a] Several departments did not list numbers of cases, so some understatement occurs in all categories.

[b] Includes six doctoral candidates located in a department initiating new program.

[c] Understated because five departments listed no estimates, and five more listed estimates for their own discipline only and inserted question marks for other disciplines.

and, as a consequence, some overstatement of the CUE-supported share. This is because: (1) some departments that do not offer a formal field of urban economics for the doctorate nevertheless have produced some dissertations which fall within the field; and (2) several departments with programs did not list doctorates, but there is evidence that they have produced some over the past five years.[7]

7. Based on an inspection of the list of doctorates completed that appears annually in the *American Economic Review*.

Table C-13 lists sources of support for doctorates in the field of urban economics. It is clear that CUE and the individual universities have been major sources of support, each furnishing roughly one-quarter of total support for doctorates over the past five years, including those now in progress.

Roughly half of the departments listed information on the level of student stipends. Eight CUE-supported departments averaged $10,000 for postdoctoral fellowships, $15,000 for postcandidacy doctoral stipends, and $6,600 for precandidacy doctoral stipends. (The postdoctoral fellowships were located at four major grant departments, so the average for those four departments was $20,000.) Fourteen other departments averaged $1,000 for postdoctoral fellowships, $2,500 for postcandidacy doctoral stipends, and $6,000 for precandidacy stipends. Of these last, four indicated that no funds were devoted to stipends.

Research

In Table C-7, average annual faculty research time was estimated as 1.32 full-time equivalent man-years (FTE) for economics departments and 1.67 FTE for business schools.

Eight of the ten CUE-supported departments furnished information on research budgets, as did ten of twenty-seven other departments. The limited response to this part of the questionnaire no doubt reflects both the confidential nature of the information and the difficulty involved in its estimation.

Research budget totals over the three-year period 1965-68 were averaged for each responding department, and then averaged over departments. (In some cases there was a good deal of year-to-year variability.) The CUE-supported departments had annual research budgets averaging roughly $80,000, of which 25 per cent was classified as educational support. The range was from $15,000 to $145,000. The budget for other departments averaged roughly $40,000, with about 7 per cent allocable to educational support and a range of from $15,000 to $80,000. It is likely that the average for this group is somewhat understated. For instance, one department did not list the dollar value of a major grant in urban economics, which is known to have been over $80,000 per year. Another listed an annual budget of $35,000, but elsewhere noted a specific grant of $275,000 over a three-year period. The inclusion of these two cases increases the estimated average budget of departments not supported by CUE to $50,000 per year.

Research budget costs per FTE man-year in research were calculated on the basis of data developed to this point. For totals listed, CUE-supported department costs were $56,300 per man-year; adjusting for the 25 per cent allocable to educational support reduced this to $42,400. Similarly, the average for other departments was $25,700 per man-year, without accounting for educational support, and $23,900 when it was taken into account. Finally, the inclusion of the two cases cited above increased average research expenditures to $30,200 per man-year.

If it is assumed that the figures of $42,400 and $30,200 hold generally for CUE-supported and other departments, respectively, then total faculty research budget can be estimated from data in Table C-6 as $1.90 million, with the

Table C-13. Sources of Support for Doctorates in Urban Economics—Detail

Source of support	Completed doctorates (1963-68)	Doctorates in progress (1968)	Total
CUE	17	27	44
University (internal)	17	19	36
University agencies	5	3	8
Federal Agencies			
U.S. Dept. of Housing and Urban Development	4	0	4
U.S. Army Corps of Engineers	1	1	2
U.S. Agency for International Development	1	0	1
Economic Development Administration	1	5	6
National Defense Education Act	0	1	1
U.S. Department of Labor	0	1	1
U.S. Air Force	0	1	1
State and local government			
California Real Estate Grant-in-Aid	3	2	5
City of Milwaukee	1	0	1
Foundations			
Ford Foundation	3	4	7
National Science Foundation	2	3	5
Carnegie Foundation	2	0	2
Wilson Foundation	1	0	1
Lingle Foundation	0	1	1
Maxwell Fellowship	0	1	1
Kaiser Foundation	0	1	1
Research Institutes, etc.			
Urban Land Institute	1	0	1
Brookings Institution	2	0	2
Atlantic Institute	0	1	1
U.S. Steel	1	0	1
Self-support	1	4	5
Not listed	11	18	29
Total	74	93	167

CUE-supported department subtotal equal to $600,000, roughly 30 per cent of the overall figure.

Research budget totals over time exhibit only a slight upward trend for individual departments, indicating that expansion of research is occurring primarily through entry of new departments and expansion in production of doctoral dissertations. Thus, of the eight responding CUE-supported departments, five show no change in budget over time, two show an increase, and one a decrease. Of the ten other departments, three show no change, four show an increase, two a decrease, and one lists information for one year only.

Data on sources of research support for 1968 appear in Table C-14, and Table C-15 lists additional sources that furnished support in the preceding years, 1966-67.

Initiation of Program and Program Problems

Departments responding to the questionnaire were asked to indicate how their program was initiated, and the role that CUE played, if any. The CUE-supported departments usually noted that their program was started through the interest of one or two faculty members, and that the CUE grant had greatly accelerated program development. In one case, the program was an outgrowth of a regional economic study.

Of the other departments, half responded to this question (fourteen of twenty-eight). The reasons cited for program initiation included: interest

Table C-14. Listed Sources of Research Support (1968)

	Number of cases		
Source of support	CUE-supported departments	Other departments	Total
CUE	10	0	10
Other grants from Resources for the Future	3	2	5
Foundations			
Ford Foundation	2	4	6
Rockefeller Foundation	0	1	1
Mellon Foundation	1	0	1
National Science Foundation	2	2	4
Federal Agencies			
U.S. Department of Housing and Urban Development	1	5	6
Public Health Service	0	3	3
Economic Development Administration	3	2	5
National Aeronautics and Space Administration	0	1	1
U.S. Army Corps of Engineers	1	0	1
Office of Economic Opportunity	1	0	1
Title 1, Higher Education Act	0	1	1
University	2	4	6
University Experiment Station	1	0	1
State government	1	4	5
Research institutes, etc.	2	1	3

and efforts of one or two faculty members (five cases); interdisciplinary interest and urban studies on campus (four cases); part of normal development, but speeded up as a result of an Economic Development Administration grant (one case); initiation through RFF research support (one case); evolution from a real estate program (one case); introduced as part of new Ph.D. program (one case); and university administration decision (one case). In this group, six departments felt that CUE had no direct influence on the establishment of a program, and one felt that it had a catalytic effect because it represented an important potential source of support.

Although no department cited student interest as a reason for the initiation of a program, some observers felt that on occasion strong student interest finally impelled a rather slow-moving faculty to introduce a program in the field.

In the survey questionnaire, a number of possible problems were listed and respondents were asked to indicate those that applied to their programs. The problems were structured in terms of discerned shortages; five areas were listed and an open category was provided to handle any other difficulties. Of course, a value judgment is involved when a respondent lists as a "shortage" a particular program feature that does not meet some implicit standard of adequacy. Table C-16 shows the number of departments that made specific complaints.

It turns out that shortage of funds was a major complaint for all groups, followed in frequency by shortage of faculty, and then by shortage of qualified students. The general pattern of response was quite similar between groups. No department foresaw too few positions for successful doctoral candidates.

The problem of a discerned shortage of qualified students was reported by about one-third of the departments. (Presumably, this involves both a quantity and a quality dimension.) There are some echoes of this in the student

Table C-15. Other Listed Sources of Research Support (1966-67)

Type of granting institution	Specific source of support
Foundations	Schalkenbach Foundation
	Sloane Foundation
Federal agencies	Housing and Home Finance Agency
	National Park Service
	U.S. Department of Labor Manpower Administration
Institutes	Battelle Institute
	Brookings Institution
	Institute for Research on Poverty
	Highway Research Board
	Society of Real Estate Appraisers
Cities and regional planning associations	City of New York
	City of Cambridge, Massachusetts
	S.W. Pennsylvania Regional Planning Commission
	New York Regional Plan Association

Table C-16. Number of Complaints, by Type and by Department Category (1968)

Kind of complaint	Number of departments making complaint			
	CUE-supported depart- ments	New depart- ments	All other	Total
Shortage of funds	8	3	14	25
Shortage of faculty	4	4	12	20
Too few qualified students	3	2	10	15
Too few positions for successful doctoral candidates	0	0	0	0
Lack of good teaching materials	3	0	7	10
Other	0	0	2[a]	2

[a] Lack of good research (1); lack of good data for research (1).

population. One former CUE Fellow noted that there was a fairly widespread belief that students in urban studies, generally, and in urban economics, in particular, were often marginal, academically. He felt that the CUE program had some upgrading impact.

PART 3. THE HISTORY OF THE COMMITTEE ON URBAN ECONOMICS

Appendix D
CUE Chronology

Events of note are briefly listed by date. The twenty-two meetings of the Committee are shown within this chronological order, noting date, locale, and joint purposes. The number of each meeting appears in parentheses.

1958 December	Program paper prepared by Harvey S. Perloff discussed need for conscious effort to advance urban economics, and capability of RFF to develop a program encouraging growth of field. Program discussed with staff members of the Ford Foundation's Program in Economic Development and Administration.
1959 Jan.-June	Series of discussions by Reuben G. Gustavson, Joseph L. Fisher, and Harvey S. Perloff with staff members of the Ford Foundation on the advancement of urban economics. Form and objectives of a committee on urban economics specified. Formal proposal to the Ford Foundation submitted February 26, 1959.
July 21	Public announcement of first Ford Foundation grant to RFF to establish an interuniversity group to advance research and education in urban economics. Amount: $375,000. Major purposes were to: 1. develop university centers in urban economics; 2. attract new talent into the field; 3. serve a clearing house function; 4. sponsor conferences; 5. assist in specific metropolitan economic studies;

		6. promote data improvement;
		7. serve a liaison function.
		RFF to serve as fiscal agent and provide secretariat for CUE.
Oct. 9	(1)	First meeting of invited members at RFF, Washington, D. C.
Dec.		Inauguration of CUE fellowship program.

1960

Jan.		Results of questionnaire survey on current research and teaching indicate field in embryonic state.
Jan. 20	(2)	Meeting at RFF, Washington, D. C.
March		First CUE fellowships awarded.
April 21-22	(3)	Meeting at Pittsburgh. Included discussion of work of Pittsburgh Economic Study.
June 16-17		Conference on Economics of Urban Migration, New York. Co-sponsored with Institute of Public Administration.
Sept. 6-7	(4)	Meeting at St. Louis. In conjunction with first Conference on Regional Accounts.
Sept. 7-8		First Conference on Regional Accounts, Washington University, St. Louis.

1961

Jan. 24	(5)	Meeting at RFF, Washington, D. C.
April 6-8		Seminar on Intrametropolitan Models, Brookings Institution, Washington, D. C.
May 12	(6)	Meeting at Minneapolis. In conjunction with discussion of Upper Midwest Economic Study.
May 18-19		First Conference on the Economics of Human Resources, RFF, Washington, D. C.
June 16-17		First Conference on Applied Urban Economics, co-sponsored with Graduate School of Business, Indiana University.
Oct. 18-19	(7)	Meeting at RFF, Washington, D. C.

1962

March 15-16	(8)	Meeting at the RAND Corporation, Santa Monica. Review and discussion of RAND Urban Transportation Study.
May 14-15		First Conference on Public Expenditure Decisions in the Urban Community, Brookings Institution, Washington, D. C.
Oct. 12		Second Conference on Applied Urban Economics, co-sponsored with Graduate School of Business, Indiana University.
Nov. 16-17		Second Conference on the Economics of Urban Human Resources, Brookings Institution, Washington, D. C.

Nov. 29	(9)	Meeting at Miami Beach. In conjunction with Second Conference on Regional Accounts.
Nov. 29-Dec. 1		Second Conference on Regional Accounts, Miami Beach, Florida.

1963

April 12	(10)	Meeting at RFF, Washington, D. C.

1964

Feb. 20	(11)	Meeting at Institute of Public Administration, New York City. In conjunction with Second Conference on Urban Public Expenditures at New York University.
Feb. 21-22		Second Conference on Urban Public Expenditures, New York University.
April 3		"A Proposal for a Five-Year Program of Research on Urban Economic Problems" submitted to the Ford Foundation.
Oct. 30		Second Ford Foundation grant announced. $900,000 awarded as terminal grant, to continue the program in urban economics under CUE over a five-year period.
Nov. 18-19	(12)	Meeting at Miami Beach. In conjunction with Third Conference on Regional Accounts.
Nov. 19-21		Third Conference on Regional Accounts, Miami Beach, Florida.

1965

Jan. 28	(13)	Meeting at RFF, Washington, D. C. Matching Grant Program established. CUE to contribute $25,000 per year for three years, matched by participating university contribution of $25,000 per year for five years.
April 1	(14)	Meeting at RFF, Washington, D. C.
May 1		Letter announcing Matching Grant Program sent to departments of economics and schools of business.
June 4		Detailed letter to nineteen universities responding favorably to letter of May 1, 1965.
Oct. 1	(15)	Meeting at RFF, Washington, D. C. Full matching grants made to five universities meeting grant conditions: University of California (Los Angeles), Indiana University, Syracuse University, Washington University (St. Louis), Wayne State University.

1966

March 25	(16)	Meeting at RFF, Washington, D. C.
April 23		Matching grant to Iowa State University ($15,000 total over three-year period) and New York University ($22,500 total over three-year period).

Oct. 27		"Information Services in Urban Economics" funded, consisting of (1) a newsletter and (2) a graduate student journal of review articles, under Charles Leven and John Martinson. Eventuated in later publication of: (1) *News in Urban Economics;* and (2) *Reviews in Urban Economics.*
		Matching grant to Brown University ($25,000 total over three-year period).
Sept. 30	(17)	Meeting at Maxwell School, Syracuse University, Syracuse, New York. Included review of the urban economics program at Syracuse under the CUE matching grant.
1967		
Jan. 26-28		Conference on Urban Economics: Analytical and Policy Issues, Shoreham Hotel, Washington, D. C. Survey of state of the field. CUE fellowship recipients invited to attend.
Jan. 27	(18)	Meeting at Shoreham Hotel, Washington, D. C. In conjunction with Conference on Urban Economics.
April 8		Matching grant to University of Pittsburgh ($26,750 total over three-year period).
Sept. 28	(19)	Meeting at St. Louis. Washington University Matching Grant Program and related programs discussed.
1968		
Jan. 24-26		Fourth Conference on Regional Accounts, University of California (Los Angeles).
Jan. 25	(20)	Meeting at Los Angeles. In conjunction with Fourth Conference on Regional Accounts. University of California (Los Angeles) matching grant and related programs discussed.
March 29	(21)	Meeting at Chicago. Matching grant program at Indiana University, urban programs at University of Illinois discussed.
		Dick Netzer elected chairman of successor committee to CUE, with anticipated completion of activity under RFF auspices.
March 29 and Oct. 4		Future of the field and role of successor committee discussed by members.
April 19		Matching grant to University of Chicago ($45,000 total over three-year period).
Oct. 4	(22)	Meeting at RFF, Washington, D. C. Final meeting under RFF auspices.
Oct. 24		Terminal grants made by RFF Board of Directors.

Appendix E
CUE Membership

During the ten-year period from 1959 to 1968, a total of thirty-two persons served on the Committee on Urban Economics. As initially constituted, the Committee consisted of fourteen members. With the advent of the second grant, it was expanded in 1965 to include nineteen members. The selection of the new members reflected a policy of broadening the Committee representation by adding members both from the field of economics and from other fields. This facilitated an expanded program of activities, obtained increased coverage of areas of specialization, and reflected the growing interest and participation in the field. Of the fourteen initial members, eleven were economists, one a political scientist, one a sociologist, and one an urban planner. In 1965, there were fourteen economists, two urban planners, one geographer, one political scientist, and one sociologist.

In 1967-68, the membership of the Committee was again expanded to a new total of twenty-seven. All eight new members were economists and in a sense represented a new wave of urban economists, indicative of the growth of the field. Five of the eight were key persons in the urban economics program at matching grant universities not then represented on the Committee; the other three were involved in research in urban economics. The expansion of the membership was of help in assessing the future role and function of CUE and in facilitating its proposed evolution into an interuniversity successor committee.

The professional affiliations of the thirty-two members of the Committee follow.

Economics (other than business administration and economic history)	20
Business administration	1
Economic history	1
Geography	1
Political science	3
Sociology	2
Urban planning	2
	32

The affiliations of the members reflect the Committee's focus on applying economics to urban problems, though with an awareness of the potential contribution of other disciplines in their solution.

As indicated in Table E-1, Perloff, as chairman, and Barnett, Fisher, Heller, Hirsch, Hoover, Ruggles, Weimer, and Wingo have served since the Committee's inception. Fitch and Schaller joined in 1960 and have served since that date. Table E-1 is followed by a list of Committee members in alphabetic order, showing for each member the period of service on the Committee, discipline, affiliation while on the Committee, and some representative scholarly publications. It can be seen that the Committee has consisted primarily of persons from the academic community; twenty-seven members were connected with universities, four with RFF, and one with a research institute.

Table E-1. Members of the Committee on Urban Economics, by period of service

Member	1959	1960	1961	1962	1963	1964	1965	1966	1967	1968
Harvey S. Perloff, chairman	X	X	X	X	X	X	X	X	X	X
Harold J. Barnett	X	X	X	X	X	X	X	X	X	X
Joseph L. Fisher	X	X	X	X	X	X	X	X	X	X
Alvin Hansen	X	X	X							
Walter W. Heller	X	X	X	X	X	X	X	X	X	X
Werner Z. Hirsch	X	X	X	X	X	X	X	X	X	X
Edgar M. Hoover	X	X	X	X	X	X	X	X	X	X
Richard Ruggles	X	X	X	X	X	X	X	X	X	X
Arthur M. Weimer	X	X	X	X	X	X	X	X	X	X
Lowdon Wingo, Jr.	X[a]	X[a]	X[a]	X[a]	X[a]	X	X	X	X	X
Robert A. Dahl		X								
Lyle C. Fitch		X	X	X	X	X	X	X	X	X
Howard G. Schaller		X	X	X	X	X	X	X	X	X
Leo F. Schnore		X	X	X	X					
Tibor Scitovsky		X								
Robert C. Wood		X	X	X	X					
Wilbur R. Thompson						X[a]	X	X	X	X
Donald J. Bogue							X	X	X	X
Alan K. Campbell							X	X	X	X
F. Stuart Chapin, Jr.							X	X	X	X
William L. Garrison							X	X	X	X
Eric E. Lampard							X	X	X	X
Julius Margolis							X	X	X	X
Selma J. Mushkin							X	X	X	X
Benjamin Chinitz									X	X
Irving Hoch									X[a]	X[a]
Charles L. Leven									X	X
John R. Meyer									X	X
Jerome W. Milliman									X	X
Dick Netzer									X	X
James Prescott									X	X
Edwin S. Mills										X

X = membership during year indicated (membership dated from first participation in CUE activities).

[a] Ex-officio membership for year indicated.

Some of the Committee members have served in government or related agencies during their tenure on the Committee. Thus, Perloff was a member of the Committee of Nine, set up by the Organization of American States to appraise Alliance for Progress plans, while Heller served as chairman of the Council of Economic Advisors. Following the period of his Committee membership, Wood has served as Under Secretary of HUD. Prior to his membership, Chinitz was Deputy Administrator, Economic Development Administration. Campbell was elected at-large delegate to the New York State Constitutional Convention where he served as chairman of the Convention Committee on Local Government and Home Rule. On the local level, Fisher is a member of the County Board of Arlington County, Virginia, and president of the Metropolitan Washington Council of Governments.

Members of the Committee on Urban Economics

This list contains information on each member of the committee, his period of service, discipline, affiliation(s) during that period in chronological order, and some representative scholarly publications.

HARVEY S. PERLOFF   (1959-68)   Economics
Chairman, Committee on Urban Economics.
Director, Regional and Urban Studies Program, Resources for the Future, Inc.
Dean, School of Architecture & Urban Planning, University of California, Los Angeles.

Education for Planning: City, State and Regional.
State and Local Finance in the National Economy (co-author).
Regions, Resources, and Economic Growth (co-author).
Issues in Urban Economics (co-editor).

HAROLD J. BARNETT   (1959-68)   Economics
Chairman, Department of Economics, Wayne State University.
Department of Economics, Washington University.

"A Proposal for Wired City Television" in *The Radio Spectrum, Its Use and Regulation* (co-author).
Scarcity and Growth (co-author).
"Specific Industry Output Projections" in *Long-Range Economic Projections.*
Energy Uses and Supplies.

DONALD J. BOGUE   (1965-68)   Sociology
Department of Sociology, University of Chicago.

"The Spread of Cities," *American Economic Review.*
Structure of the Metropolitan Community.
Population of the United States.
Economic Areas of the United States.

ALAN K. CAMPBELL   (1965-68)   Political Science
Director, Metropolitan Studies Program, Syracuse University.
"Taxes and Industrial Organization in the N.Y. Metropolitan Region,"
National Tax Journal.
"Public Policy for Urban America" in *Issues in Urban Economics* (co-author).
"The Metropolitan Education Dilemma: Matching Resources to Needs,"
Urban Affairs Quarterly (co-author).
Metropolitan America: Fiscal Patterns and Governmental Systems (co-author).

F. STUART CHAPIN, JR.   (1965-68)   Planning
Department of City and Regional Planning, University of North Carolina,
Chapel Hill.
Cultural Change.
Urban Growth Dynamics in a Regional Cluster of Cities (co-author).
Urban Land Use Planning.
Household Activity Systems (co-author).

BENJAMIN CHINITZ   (1967-68)   Economics
Chairman, Department of Economics, Brown University.
Freight and the Metropolis.
City and Suburb; The Economics of Metropolitan Growth (editor).
"Contrasts in Agglomeration: New York and Pittsburgh," *American Economic Review.*
Region in Transition (co-author). (Volume 1 of the Pittsburgh Regional Economic Study.)

ROBERT A. DAHL   (1960)   Political Science
Chairman, Department of Political Science, Yale University.
Who Governs? Democracy and Power in an American City.
Politics, Economics, and Welfare.
A Preface to Democratic Theory.
Political Opposition in Western Democracies.

JOSEPH L. FISHER   (1959-68)   Economics
President, Resources for the Future, Inc.
"Natural Resources and Technological Change," *Land Economics.*
"Research in Regional Economic Growth" in *Problems in the Study of Economic Growth.*
World Prospects for Natural Resources (co-author).
Resources in America's Future (co-author).

LYLE C. FITCH   (1960-68)   Economics
President, Institute of Public Administration.
"Goals for Urban Development" in *Urban America: Goals and Problems.*
"National Development and National Policy" in *Environment and Policy: The Next Fifty Years.*
Political and Fiscal Problems of Metropolitan Areas.
Urban Transportation and Public Policy.

WILLIAM L. GARRISON   (1965-68)   Geography
The Transportation Center, Northwestern University.
Director, The Center for Urban Studies, University of Illinois at Chicago Circle.
  Studies of Highway Development and Geographic Change.
  Spatial Structure of the Economy.
  "Factor-analytic Study of the Connectivity of a Transportation Network"
      (co-author), *Regional Science Association Papers.*
  "Values of Regional Science," *Regional Science Association Papers.*

ALVIN HANSEN   (1959-63)   Economics
Professor of Political Economy Emeritus, Harvard University.
  The American Economy.
  Business Cycles and National Income.
  Economic Policy and Full Employment.
  Urban Redevelopment and Housing (co-author).

WALTER W. HELLER   (1959-68)   Economics
Chairman, Department of Economics, University of Minnesota.
Chairman, Council of Economic Advisers.
Department of Economics, University of Minnesota.
  Savings in the Modern Economy.
  Taxes and Fiscal Policy in Underdeveloped Countries.
  Revenue Sharing and the City.
  New Dimensions of Political Economy.

WERNER Z. HIRSCH   (1959-68)   Economics
Department of Economics, Washington University.
Director, Institute of Government and Public Affairs, University of California,
Los Angeles.
  Analysis of the Rising Costs of Public Education.
  "Interindustry Relations of a Metropolitan Area," *Review of Economics and
      Statistics.*
  Regional Accounts for Policy Decisions (editor).
  "Input-Output Techniques for Urban Government Decisions," *American
      Economic Review.*

IRVING HOCH   (1967-68)   Economics
Resources for the Future, Inc.
  "Simultaneous Equation Bias in the Context of the Cobb-Douglas Production
      Function," *Econometrica*
  Forecasting Economic Activity for the Chicago Region.
  "Estimating Efficient Spacing for Arterials and Expressways" in *Traffic Origin
      and Destination Studies, Appraisal of Methods* (co-author).
  "Economic Analysis of Wilderness Areas" in *Wilderness and Recreation.*

EDGAR M. HOOVER   (1959-68)   Economics
Center for Regional Economic Studies,
  Department of Economics, University of Pittsburgh.
  Location of Economic Activity.
  Population and Economic Growth in Low-Income Countries (co-author).

Anatomy of a Metropolis (co-author).

"Motor Metropolis: Urban Transportation in America," *Journal of Industrial Economics.*

ERIC E. LAMPARD   (1965-68)   Economic History
Graduate Program in Economic History, University of Wisconsin, Madison.
   "Historical Aspects of Urbanization" in *Study of Urbanization.*
   "Urbanization and Social Change" in *The Historian and the City.*
   "The History of Cities in Economically Advanced Areas," *Economic Development and Cultural Change.*
   "The Evolving System of Cities in the U. S." in *Issues in Urban Economics.*

CHARLES L. LEVEN   (1967-68)   Economics
Director, Institute for Urban and Regional Studies;
Department of Economics, Washington University.
   "Measuring the Economic Base," *Papers and Proceedings of the Regional Science Association*
   "Regional Income and Product Accounts" in *Design of Regional Accounts.*
   "An Economist Looks at Urban Renewal," *Journal of Housing.*
   Design of a National System of Regional Accounts (co-author).

JULIUS MARGOLIS   (1965-68)   Economics
Department of Economics, Stanford University.
   "Welfare Criteria, Pricing and Decentralization of Public Services," *Quarterly Journal of Economics.*
   Northern California's Water Industry (co-author).
   The Public Economy of Urban Communities (editor).
   "The Demand for Urban Public Services" in *Issues in Urban Economics.*

JOHN R. MEYER   (1967-68)   Economics
Department of Economics, Harvard University.
   "Economics of Slavery in the Ante-bellum South," *Journal of Political Economy.*
   "Economics of Competition" in *Transportation Industry.*
   The Investment Decision.
   The Urban Transportation Problem (co-author).

JEROME W. MILLIMAN   (1967-68)   Economics
Director, Institute for Applied Urban Economics, Indiana University.
   "Land Values as Measures of Primary Irrigation Benefits," *Journal of Farm Economics.*
   "Water Law and Private Decision-making: A Critique," *Journal of Law and Economics.*
   Water Supply: Economics, Technology and Policy (co-author).
   Systems Simulation for Regional Analysis (co-author).

EDWIN S. MILLS   (1968)   Economics
Chairman, Department of Political Economy, Johns Hopkins University.
   Price, Output and Inventory Policy.
   "A Study of Optimum Assembly Runs," *Operations Research.*

72

"An Aggregate Model of Resource Allocation in a Metropolitan Area," *American Economic Review.*
"The Value of Land" in *The Quality of the Urban Environment.*

SELMA J. MUSHKIN   (1965-68)   Economics
State-Local Finances Project,
George Washington University;
The Urban Institute
  "Investment in People Through Health," *Supplement to Journal of Political Economy.*
  "Barriers to A System of Federal Grants in Aid," *National Tax Journal.*
  Economics of Higher Education.
  An Operative PPB System (co-author).

DICK NETZER   (1967-68)   Economics
Chairman, Department of Economics, New York University
  Economics of the Property Tax.
  Financing Government in New York City (co-author).
  "Housing Taxation and Housing Policy" in *The Economic Problems of Housing.*
  Public Services in Older Cities (co-author).

JAMES R. PRESCOTT   (1967-68)   Economics
Department of Economics, Iowa State University.
  "Rental Formation in Federally Supported Public Housing," *Land Economics.*
  Public Housing: A Project Analysis.

RICHARD RUGGLES   (1959-68)   Economics
Chairman, Department of Economics, Yale University.
  National Income Accounts and Income Analysis (co-author).
  "Relation of the Undergraduate Major to Graduate Economics," *American Economic Review.*
  "The U. S. National Accounts and Their Development," *American Economic Review.*
  "The Value of Value Theory," *American Economic Review.*

HOWARD G. SCHALLER   (1960-68)   Economics
Dean, School of Business Administration, Tulane University;
International Business Research Institute, Indiana University.
  "Social Security Transfer Payments and Differences in State Per Capita Incomes, 1929, 1939 and 1949," *Review of Economics and Statistics.*
  "Federal Grants in Aid," *National Tax Journal.*
  Public Expenditure Decisions in the Urban Economy (editor).

LEO F. SCHNORE   (1960-63)   Sociology
Department of Sociology, University of Wisconsin, Madison.
  "Social Morphology and Human Ecology," *American Journal of Sociology.*
  "Statistical Measurement of Urbanization and Economic Development," *Land Economics.*

"Social Mobility in Demographic Perspective," *American Sociological Review*.

Study of Urbanization (editor).

TIBOR SCITOVSKY   (1960)   Economics

Department of Economics, University of California, Berkeley.

Welfare and Competition.

Mobilizing Resources for War.

Economic Theory and Western European Integration.

"Standards for the Performance of our Economic System," *American Economic Review*.

WILBUR R. THOMPSON   (1964-68)   Economics

Department of Economics, Wayne State University.

"Residential Service Construction: A Study of Induced Investment," *Review of Economics and Statistics*.

"Measurement of the Economic Base of the Metropolitan Area," *Land Economics*.

Econometric Model of Postwar State Industrial Development.

A Preface to Urban Economics.

ARTHUR M. WEIMER   (1959-68)   Business Administration

Dean, School of Business, Indiana University;

Special Assistant to the President, Indiana University.

Principles of Real Estate (co-author).

Business Administration: An Introductory Management Approach.

Investors in Downtown Real Estate.

LOWDON WINGO, JR.   (1959-68)   Planning

Resources for the Future, Inc.

"Natural Resource Endowment and Regional Economic Growth" in *Natural Resources and Economic Growth* (co-author).

Transportation and Urban Land.

Cities and Space (editor).

Issues in Urban Economics (co-editor).

ROBERT C. WOOD   (1960-63)   Political Science

Department of Economics and Social Science, Massachusetts Institute of Technology.

Joint Center for Urban Studies, Massachusetts Institute of Technology—Harvard University.

Suburbia: Its People and Their Politics.

Metropolis Against Itself.

1400 Governments.

Appendix F
CUE Advisory Committees

In its orientation and in its operation, CUE defined a number of areas of specialization within the field of urban economics. It found scholarly leadership to spearhead its activities in each subarea, including the support or organization of committees to advise it of developments and opportunities in the respective subareas and to carry out programs to help advance the development of those subareas. These advisory committees were the Committee on Regional Accounts (CORA); the Committee on Urban Public Economics (COUPE);[1] and the Committee on Urban Human Resources.

In 1958, through its regional studies program, RFF gave financial support to a program of regional accounts. After the formation of CUE in 1959, this regional accounts program was constituted as CORA, under the chairmanship of Werner Hirsch, and became formally associated with the urban economics program. A number of CORA members also served on CUE.

The aim of CORA was to promote the establishment of a system of urban and regional accounts similar to that used since the 1930s in the analysis of the national economy. It co-ordinated its work through periodic conferences and through less formal meetings during the year. By 1965, the committee felt that sufficient data had been gathered and methodology developed to justify concentrating future efforts on two projects that would attempt to translate theory into practice. They were: (1) the construction of a uniform system of regional accounts for the United States as a whole, and (2) the development of a regional data bank and information system. These projects were under the direction, respectively, of Charles Leven and Werner Z. Hirsch. Both enterprises were supported by CUE.

Four major conferences took place under the auspices of CORA (in 1960, 1962, 1964, and 1968). In addition, members of CORA participated in sessions on regional accounts sponsored by the American Statistical Association (1960 year-end meeting) and the American Economic Association (1961 and 1967 year-end meetings).

In January 1968, the members of CORA decided that the committee had accomplished its objectives and therefore voted to discontinue committee operations and establish a successor organization, to be called the Conference on Regional Accounts. The Conference, composed of about twenty members

1. COUPE was originally named the Committee on Urban Public Expenditures; its name was changed in 1966.

from universities, private research organizations, and government, plans to sponsor semiannual meetings devoted to matters relevant to regional accounts, with emphasis on governmental decisions and information in urban areas. At its final meeting, CUE allocated funds for the ongoing activities of the Conference.

The Committee on Urban Public Expenditures and the Committee on Urban Human Resources were both established as subcommittees of CUE. Each contained a number of members who were not members of CUE.

COUPE, under the chairmanship of Julius Margolis, sponsored research on state and local services, finances, and the structure of urban regional governments. Two major conferences were devoted to urban public expenditures (1962 and 1965), and in recent years, semiannual research seminars have surveyed critical areas of policy and analysis in the urban public economy. The change of name to the Committee on Urban Public Economics coincided with the evolution of COUPE into an ongoing committee in its own right. At its final meeting, CUE allocated funds to support future activities of COUPE.

Unlike CORA and COUPE, which both developed independent programs, the Committee on Urban Human Resources served CUE essentially in an advisory capacity. Two conferences on urban human resources were held (in 1961 and 1962), and the subcommittee provided CUE with some useful technical memoranda. The limited results, relative to the consequences flowing from the organization of the other advisory committees, reflect the limited development of the area of urban human resources. Although the CUE secretariat attempted to identify leading scholars in this emergent subfield and to establish communication links among them, the effort was not particularly successful, as little cohesion and community of interest emerged.

Details on the conferences noted here appear in Appendix J. Conference participants are listed in Appendix M. A listing of the members of the advisory committees follows. This includes all persons who served on those committees.

Members of the Committee on Regional Accounts (CORA)

Werner Z. Hirsch, University of California, Los Angeles, California (*chairman*)
Harold J. Barnett, Washington University
George H. Borts, Brown University
Alfred Eisenpreis,* Allied Stores Corporation
Karl Fox,* Iowa State University
Douglas Greenwald, McGraw-Hill Publishing Company
Edgar M. Hoover, University of Pittsburgh
Nathan Koffsky,* U. S. Department of Agriculture
Charles L. Leven, Washington University
Herman Miller, U. S. Bureau of the Census
Harvey S. Perloff, Resources for the Future, Inc.
Richard Ruggles,* Yale University
Sidney Sonenblum, National Planning Association, Washington, D. C., and
    University of California, Los Angeles

---

* Member during part of the period of committee's existence.

Members of the Committee on Urban Public Expenditures (COUPE)

Julius Margolis, Stanford University (*chairman*)
Harvey E. Brazer, University of Michigan
James Buchanan,* University of California, Los Angeles
Jesse Burkhead, Syracuse University
Anthony Downs, Real Estate Research Corporation, Chicago
John Dyckman, University of California, Berkeley
Otto Eckstein,* Harvard University
Lyle C. Fitch,* Institute of Public Administration
Roland N. McKean, University of Virginia
Jerome W. Milliman, Indiana University
Richard A. Musgrave, Harvard University
Dick Netzer, New York University
Jerome Rothenberg, Northwestern University
Howard G. Schaller,* Indiana University
Burton A. Weisbrod, University of Wisconsin
William Vickrey, Columbia University

---

* Member during part of the period of committee's existence.

Members of the Committee on Urban Human Resources

Mark Perlman, University of Pittsburgh (*chairman*)
Robert L. Aronson, Cornell University
Gary S. Becker, National Bureau of Economic Research
Neil W. Chamberlain, Yale University
Henry Cohen, The Mayor's Office, New York City
H. M. Douty, U. S. Bureau of Labor Statistics
William Goldner, University of California, Berkeley
W. Lee Hansen, University of California, Los Angeles
F. Ray Marshall, University of Texas
Jacob Mincer, National Bureau of Economic Research
Richard F. Muth, Washington University
Leo F. Schnore, University of Wisconsin
Martin Segal, Dartmouth University
Burton A. Weisbrod, University of Wisconsin

Appendix G
CUE Expenditures

Over its ten-year life, CUE spent 1.37 million dollars. The breakdown of these expenditures by category appears in Table G-1. The matching grant program allocations amounted to 37 per cent of the total, exclusive of CUE administrative costs for organizing and operating the program, and spending for the fellowship program comprised 12 per cent, so that direct educational expenditures made up roughly half the budget. Research and communication grants were slightly under 25 per cent of the total; while compensation, travel, and other expenses made up about 20 per cent. (A large portion of the compensation item was, in effect, CUE research expenditure. See "Research at Resources for the Future," Appendix H.) Finally, roughly 8 per cent is categorized as "terminal grants covering balance," and consists of funds allocated to carry on

Table G-1. CUE Expenditures by Category

Expenditure	Amount	Percentage of total
Compensation and employee benefits[a]	$ 182,245.69	13.3%
Travel[b]	75,686.08	5.5
Other expenses	27,698.44	2.0
Fellowships	163,117.68	11.9
Matching grants	509,250.00	37.0
Research grants	250,924.00	18.3
Communication grants	61,150.00	4.4
Terminal grants covering balance	104,453.80	7.6
Grand total[c] (as of 1/31/69)	$1,374,525.69	100.0

[a] Includes two years of compensation to Wilbur Thompson and two and one-half years compensation to Irving Hoch plus a fraction of the compensation of Harvey S. Perloff, Lowdon Wingo, Jr., and secretarial and clerical assistance. See "Research at Resources for the Future" in Appendix H.

[b] Includes travel expenses of CUE members to CUE meetings and travel expenses of conference participants to conferences sponsored by CUE.

[c] Consists of $364,631.29 expended in first grant period and $1,009,894.40 expended in second grant period. The latter figure includes $10,368.71 carried over to the second period from the first grant. Some minor adjustments in this table's values will occur, reflecting small increments in interest income after January 31, 1969, and some estimated values appearing in some cost items.

78

operations begun under CUE auspices, including the operations of the successor committee.

The grand total of 1.37 million dollars is the sum of the first grant of $375,000, the second grant of $900,000, and interest earned on unexpended funds.

Table G-2 lists expenditures by category for each grant period. Tables G-3, G-4, G-5, and G-6 break each category down to its component items, over time, and cover, in turn, research grants, communication grants, matching grants, and terminal grants.

Table G-2. CUE Expenditures over the Two Grant Periods, by Category

Expenditure	First grant period (Oct. 1, 1959-Sept. 30, 1964)	Second grant period (Oct. 1, 1964-Sept. 30, 1969)
Compensation and employee benefits	$ 78,435.19	$ 103,810.50
Travel	40,677.33	35,008.75
Other expenses	10,365.65	17,332.79
Fellowships	92,705.12	70,412.56[a]
Matching grants	–	509,250.00
Research grants	124,848.00[b]	126,076.00
Communication grants	17,600.00[c]	43,550.00
Total expenditures (excluding terminal grants)	364,631.29	905,440.60
Balance carried forward	10,368.71	–
Terminal grants	–	104,453.80[d]
Grand total	$375,000.00	$1,009,894.40[e]

[a] $71,412.56 allocated, $1,000 refund obtained.

[b] Includes refunds in part of two grants: Northwestern University refund of $1,646 on grant of $8,200 and Duke University refund of $447 on grant of $8,087.

[c] Includes refund of $2,500 from the University of Pennsylvania for seminar grant. Seminar held but grant not used.

[d] Subject to minor adjustments reflecting some estimated values under other expenses and terminal grants and the possibility of some additional income earned on CUE funds after January 31, 1969.

[e] The sources of CUE funds in the second grant period were:

$900,000.00 Grant Sept. 30, 1964
  10,368.71 Balance first grant
  26,260.24 Income from investments Oct. 1, 1964-Sept. 30, 1965
  29,159.62 Income from investments Oct. 1, 1965-Sept. 30, 1966
  26,102.83 Income from investments Oct. 1, 1966-Sept. 30, 1967
  15,815.00 Income from investments Oct. 1, 1967-Sept. 30, 1968
   2,188.00 Income from investments Oct. 1, 1968-Jan. 30, 1969

Some small additional income from investments will be earned after January 31, 1969, and prior to final disposition of all grants.

Table G-3. CUE Research Grants

First grant period	
October 1, 1959-September 30, 1960	
National Planning Association	
Preparation of regional economic projections.	$ 11,250
Washington University	
Study of the value of human capital of a community	
as a social welfare indicator.	1,390
Wayne State University	
Study on the collection and organization of economic data in	
the major metropolitan areas, with a focus on Southern Michigan.	12,000
October 1, 1960-September 30, 1961	
California, University of	
Study of analytical problems and policy issues	
in the economics of housing and urban land use.	2,706
Chicago, University of	
Study of the effect on property values of population	
characteristics related to urban redevelopment.	3,295
Wayne State University	
Study on analysis of growth and cycle patterns and	
income distribution in metropolitan areas.	2,185
October 1, 1961-September 30, 1962	
California, University of	
An analysis of intraurban consumer spatial behavior.	4,163
Northwestern University	
Study of the core area as a metropolitan supply center grant $8,200	
for business services. refund —1,646	6,554
Kentucky Research Foundation	
Study of patterns of consumption among urban families.	3,350
London, University of	
Preparation of benefit-cost analysis and theoretical	
material to complete book on urban problems.	10,340
Morgan State College	
A survey design for an analysis of the Negro housing market.	1,775
National Planning Association	
Preparation of metropolitan area economic projections.	30,000
Institute of Public Administration	
Probability planning and administration.	19,030
October 1, 1962-September 30, 1964	
Brown University	
Study of the status and migration of the urban Negro.	8,500
Duke University	
Urban population redistribution and changes in the grant $8,087	
journey to work. refund —447	7,640
Canisius College	
Study of national metropolitan area financial relations.	670
First grant period total	$124,848

Second grant period

October 1, 1964-September 30, 1965
  California, University of
    Development of a regional data bank and information
    system for Southern California.   39,888
  Chicago, University of
    The changing spatial structure of metropolitan areas.   17,000
  Washington University
    Development of techniques for regional social accounts.   41,450
  Wayne State University
    Economic analysis of the "system of cities."   20,018

October 1, 1965-September 30, 1966
  California, University of
    Housing market analysis.   4,437

October 1, 1966-September 30, 1967
  California, University of
    Supplemental grant for housing market analysis.   245

October 1, 1967-September 30, 1968
  New York University
    An overview of the field of public assistance as
    related to urban problems.   3,038

    Second grant period total $126,076

Table G-4. CUE Communication Grants

First grant period

1959-60
  Pennsylvania, University of
    Meeting for development of metropolitan spatial
    transportation models. $ 800
1960-61
  Joint Center for Urban Studies of the
  Massachusetts Institute of Technology and
  Harvard University
    Study on improvement of sources for urban economic research.   5,000
1962-64
  Indiana University
    Conference on applied urban economics.   1,500
  Illinois, University of
    Survey of urban and regional education and
    research in American universities.   10,000
  Illinois, University of
    Supplemental grant for completion of survey of
    urban and regional studies at U.S. universities.   300
  Pennsylvania, University of   grant $2,500
    Seminar on models of land use development.   refund —2,500   –
    (Seminar held but grant not used)

    First grant period total $17,600

Second grant period

1964-65
  Stanford University
    An analysis of research needs for the study of
    cost functions of urban public services $ 4,250
1965-66
  Illinois, University of
    Expansion and improvement of periodical *Research Digest.* $ 9,300
1966-67
  George Washington University
    Interuniversity exchange of research on
    cost-effectiveness studies in urban economics.   –
    (A grant of $10,000 was made but the principal
    investigator, Selma Mushkin, joined the Urban
    Institute in 1968. The project was then
    terminated and the grant returned to RFF.)
  Stanford University
    Seminar meeting of Committee on Urban Public Economics.   18,000
  Washington University
    Information services in urban economics.   12,000

      Second grant period total $43,550

Table G-5. Matching Grants

Second grant period

Oct. 1, 1965-Sept. 30, 1966
  University of California, Los Angeles
    Research and education in urban economics. $ 75,000
  Indiana University
    Research and education in urban economics.   75,000
  Iowa State University
    Workshop in urban economics.   15,000
  New York University
    Workshop in urban economics.   22,500
  Syracuse University
    Research and education in urban economics.   75,000
  Washington University
    Research and education in urban economics.   75,000
  Wayne State University
    Research and education in urban economics.   75,000

Oct. 1, 1966-Sept. 30, 1967
  Brown University
    Research and education in urban economics. $ 25,000
  University of Pittsburgh
    Training and research programs in urban economics.   26,750

Oct. 1, 1967-Sept. 30, 1968
  University of Chicago
    Research and education in urban economics.   45,000

      Total $509,250

Table G-6. Terminal Grants

Interuniversity committee on urban economics (successor to CUE)—terminal grant[a]	$ 50,000.00
Conference on Regional Accounts (successor organization to Committee on Regional Accounts)[b]	17,600.00
Committee on Urban Public Economics, ongoing activities[b]	17,984.33
Estimated production and distribution costs, CUE Report	5,000.00
Estimated supplementary grants[a]	13,869.47
Total	$104,453.80

[a] CUE recommended to RFF that $5,000 be reserved to support a conference on the use of regional information systems, if such a conference eventuated. In addition, it was recommended that any residual balance in CUE funds be turned over to the successor committee. As of January 31, 1969, the total available for these supplementary grants was $13,869.47. Some minor adjustments in this figure are to be expected, by way of small amounts of additional income from investments, and the appearance of some estimated figures under expenses.

[b] Discussed in Appendix F.

Appendix H
CUE Research Grants

The Committee on Urban Economics supported twenty-one research projects through a series of research grants. (In some cases more than one grant was made to a specific project.) As is probably typical, a considerable gestation period generally occurred between the initiation and the completion of research. Often, too, there was a considerable reduction in the scope of the individual study between the research proposal and the completed research product.

Ten of the fourteen supported research projects of CUE's first grant period have eventuated in some form of publication. Of the remainder, three of four will probably emerge in some published form; the fourth appears to have culminated in an unpublished interim report. Of the seven second-period grants, five have led to a book or a book manuscript now under review; one to two articles submitted for publication; and one to a manuscript now under review.

Table H-1 summarizes the status of results for the research grants as of December 1968. Detailed information on individual grants, again as of December 1968, is then presented.

Table H-1. Summary of Research Projects: Status of Results (as of 1968)

	1960	1961	1962	1963	1964	1965	1966	1967	1968
No. of grants	3	5	4	2	3	2	0	1[a]	1
Published results to 1968									
Book		1			1				
Section of book	1								
Series of reports	1								
Journal article	1	4		1					
Mimeo. final report			1						
Unpublished results (as of 1968)									
Book or section in review			1		2	1		1	
Book being prepared			1					1	
Articles in process			1			2[b]			
Mimeo. progress report				1					
Mss. under review									1

[a] Initial work on project eventuated in a "section of book in review." Later work involves a book in preparation. Hence, two results are listed for one grant.

[b] One project resulted in two journal articles that have been submitted for publication.

84

Individual Grant Information[1]

Research grants are described in terms of institution receiving grant; person(s) engaged in research; amount and date of grant; objectives; and results.

1. NATIONAL PLANNING ASSOCIATION

(Gerhard Colm and Sidney Sonenblum)

   a. $11,250 (1960)   Preparation of regional economic projections.

   b. $30,000 (1961)   Preparation of metropolitan area economic projections.

Objective. To prepare projections of important economic aggregates and indices from NPA state projections and carry out additional basic research necessary to improve metropolitan area projections.

Results. The establishment of a continuing series of metropolitan projections made available in a number of publications since 1962. For example, National Planning Association, Center for Economic Projections. *Metropolitan Area Industry, Employment and Population Estimates, 1950, 1957, 1960, 1962.* Report No. 64-VI. Washington, November 1964. ———. *The Economies of Fifteen Metropolitan Areas: Historical and Projected Employment, Output, Population, and Personal Income, 1950, 1957, 1960, 1962, and 1975.* Report No. 65-III. Washington, November 1965. ———. *Economic and Demographic Projections for Eighty-Two Metropolitan Areas.* Report No. 66-R-I. Washington, May 1966.

2. WASHINGTON UNIVERSITY   (Burton A. Weisbrod)

   $1,390 (1960)   The value of human capital of a community as a social welfare indicator.

Objective. To develop the concept of value of human capital as the discounted stream of expected incomes of the worker. Seen as a better welfare measure than per capita income.

Results. Burton Weisbrod. "An Expected-Income Measure of Economic Welfare." *Journal of Political Economy,* August 1962. See also: ———. "Valuation of Human Capital." *Journal of Political Economy,* October 1962. ———. "Education and Investment in Human Capital." *Journal of Political Economy,* October 1962, part 2.

3. WAYNE STATE UNIVERSITY

(King Adamson, Wilbur R. Thompson, John M. Mattila)

   a. $12,000 (1960)   Study on the collection and organization of economic data in major metropolitan areas.

   b. $ 2,185 (1961)   An analysis of growth and cycle patterns and income distribution in metropolitan areas.

   c. $20,018 (1964)   Economic analysis of the "system of cities."

Objective. To quantify growth and income patterns of large metropolitan areas, and analyze the network of relationships among urban centers.

---

1. Financial summaries of these items appear in Appendix Table G-3 in slightly different order.

Results. Wilbur R. Thompson. "Internal and External Factors in the Development of Urban Economies." John M. Mattila and Wilbur R. Thompson. "Appendix: Toward an Econometric Model of Urban Economics Development." Both in *Issues in Urban Economics,* edited by Harvey S. Perloff and Lowdon Wingo, Jr. Baltimore: The Johns Hopkins Press for Resources for the Future, 1968. Work used in sections of Wilbur R. Thompson. *A Preface to Urban Economics.* Baltimore: The Johns Hopkins Press for Resources for the Future, 1965.

4. UNIVERSITY OF CHICAGO   (Martin J. Bailey)
   $3,295 (1961)   The effect on property values of population characteristics related to urban redevelopment.

Objective. An attempt to identify the nature of, extent, and remedy for the effects of slums or low-income residential areas on neighboring property values for different kinds of property.

Results. Martin J. Bailey. "Effects of Race and of Other Demographic Factors on the Values of Single-Family Homes." *Land Economics,* May 1966.

5. UNIVERSITY OF CALIFORNIA, BERKELEY   (A. H. Schaaf)
   $2,706 (1961)   Study of analytical problems and policy issues in the economics of housing and land use.

Objective. To examine distributional and efficiency effects of subsidies in urban renewal.

Results. A. H. Schaaf. "Public Policies in Urban Renewal: An Economic Analysis of Justifications and Effects." *Land Economics,* February 1964. (Reprinted as *Reprint Number 36,* Center for Real Estate and Urban Economics, Institute of Urban and Regional Development, University of California, Berkeley.)

6. UNIVERSITY OF CALIFORNIA, LOS ANGELES   (David L. Huff)
   $4,163 (1961)   An analysis of intraurban consumer spatial behavior.

Objective. To develop and test some hypotheses to account for variations in consumer travel behavior, resulting from (1) socioeconomic differences among consumers, (2) variations in commodity purchases, and (3) differences in size, character, and proximity of existing urban retail facilities.

Results. David L. Huff, assisted by John W. Haggerty. *Determination of Intra-Urban Retail Trade Areas.* Los Angeles: University of California, Real Estate Research Program, 1962.

7. KENTUCKY RESEARCH FOUNDATION   (Harold W. Guthrie)
   $3,350 (1961)   Study of patterns of consumption among urban families.

Objective. To assess impact of income payments to and consumption by retired persons in metropolitan areas.

Results. Harold W. Guthrie. "The Retired Population—Boon or Burden for Local Economies." *The Quarterly Review of Economics and Business.* Urbana: University of Illinois, Bureau of Economic and Business Research, Spring 1964.

8. NORTHWESTERN UNIVERSITY, TRANSPORTATION CENTER
(Leon Moses and George Bleile [deceased])

$6,554 (1961)   The core area as a metropolitan supply center for business services.

($8,200, original grant;
$1,646, refund)

Objective. To provide insight into the development of large, core-dominated cities and into the factors affecting the location of economic activity within them.

Results. Leon Moses and Harold F. Williamson, Jr. "The Location of Economic Activity in Cities." *American Economic Review,* May 1967.

9. UNIVERSITY OF LONDON   (Nathaniel Lichfield)

$10,340 (1962)   Cost-benefit analysis in urban problems.

Objective. To develop and apply cost-benefit analysis in a variety of problem areas and at different stages in the decision-making process.

Results. Detailed cost-benefit analyses have been carried out for a series of new and redevelopment projects in various parts of the British Isles. These case studies are being published as they are completed, and a book manuscript is in preparation.

10. MORGAN STATE COLLEGE   (Homer E. Favor)

$1,775 (1962)   A survey design for the analysis of the Negro housing market.

Objective. To develop a method to facilitate identification and study of the non-white housing market as distinguished from the overall housing market.

Results. Homer E. Favor. "An Inquiry into the Delineation and Study of the Non-White Housing Market." Baltimore: Morgan State College, 1963. (Mimeo).

11. INSTITUTE OF PUBLIC ADMINISTRATION   (Ruth P. Mack)

$19,030 (1962)   Probability planning and administration.

Objective. To develop more effective techniques for the treatment of uncertainty in the projection of aspects of urban development and in the construction of urban and metropolitan policies.

Results. Draft of a book, "Planning on Uncertainty," under revision.

12. BROWN UNIVERSITY   (Richard D. Raymond)

$8,500 (1962)   Study of the status and migration of the urban Negro.

Objective. To analyze the economic determinants of the migration of the urban Negro and the economic impact of such migration.

Results. Results will be submitted in the form of several journal articles; one already submitted.

13. DUKE UNIVERSITY   (H. H. Winsborough)
    $7,640 (1963)   Urban population distribution and changes in the
                         journey to work.
    ($8,087, original grant;
    $447, refund)

Objective. To analyze the relationship between changes in urban area population concentration and changes in the distance and time of the journey to work in American cities.

Results. An interim report on the findings was prepared, entitled "Population Deconcentration and the Journey to Work." Although a monograph was initially planned, it appears that the interim report will be the culminating document of the project.

14. CANISIUS COLLEGE   (Donald J. Curran)
    $670 (1963)   Study of national-metropolitan area financial relations.

Objective. To examine the growth of federal grants going to urban metropolitan areas, with focus on effect on local spending, on the federal system, and on metropolitan awareness.

Results. Donald J. Curran. "Federal-Local Financial Relations." *Review of Social Economy,* Spring 1968.

15. UNIVERSITY OF CALIFORNIA, LOS ANGELES   (Werner Z. Hirsch)
    $39,888 (1964)   Development of a regional data bank and information system for California.

Objective. To develop and implement an information system for the State of California for use in determining information needed in solving critical state problems.

Results. Report presented and reviewed at CORA Conference, University of California, Los Angeles, January 24-26, 1968. Book draft under revision. Preliminary publications: Werner Z. Hirsch and Sidney Sonenblum. *Design of Regional Information Systems* (DORIS). Lawrence H. Revzan and J. Michael Kavanagh. *Sources of Information Relevant to California's Water, Recreation, Transportation, Education and Housing Programs.* Los Angeles: University of California, Institute of Government and Public Affairs, 1967.

16. WASHINGTON UNIVERSITY   (Charles Leven)
    $41,450 (1965)   Development of techniques for regional social accounts.

Objective. To design a system for empirical implementation of a unified set of regional accounts in both interregional and intertemporal application.

Results. Report presented and reviewed at CORA Conference, University of California, Los Angeles, January 24-26, 1968. Book draft under revision. A series of preliminary publications have been issued by the Institute for Urban and Regional Studies, Washington University, St. Louis, designated DRA (Design of Regional Accounts) reports. These are: DRA 1, "Physical Characteristics of

Cities and Regional Growth"; DRA 2, "The Size and Distribution of the Tax Base Relative to Regional Economic Growth"; DRA 3, "An Analysis of Tax Structure, Public Service Levels and Regional Economic Growth"; DRA 4, "Patterns of Population Density in St. Louis"; DRA 5, "Discussion of Some Factors Affecting Labor Productivity"; DRA 6, "Alternate Measures of Fiscal Capacity"; DRA 7, "Three Papers on Quality of Urban Environment"; DRA 8, "The Responsiveness of State Tax Revenue to Economic Growth"; and DRA 9, "Design of a National System of Regional Accounts."

17. UNIVERSITY OF CHICAGO

(Donald J. Bogue, Stephen Taber, and Terry Nichols)
$17,000 (1965)   The comparative study of the spatial structure of American metropolises.

Objective. To develop a better understanding of intraurban land use patterns through analysis of small-area data.

Results. Census tract data for all 170 metropolitan areas (1960 Census) and for 40 metropolitan areas (1950 Census) have been organized on computer tape. Two articles have been submitted for possible publication. Donald J. Bogue, "The Measurement of Segregation." Donald J. Bogue and Terry Nichols, "An Empirical System for Analyzing Metropolitan Spatial Structure."

18. UNIVERSITY OF CALIFORNIA, BERKELEY   (Wallace F. Smith)
$4,682 (1965)   Preparation of a textbook on housing market problems drawing upon contemporary theory on metropolitan development.
($4,437, original grant;
$245, supplemental
[1966])

Objective. To develop a text on housing which will serve as an introduction to economic reasoning for persons concerned with housing, and to housing issues for persons trained in economics.

Results. Draft of a book, "Housing Economics: An Introduction," completed and under review.

19. NEW YORK UNIVERSITY   (Peter S. Albin)
$3,038 (1968)   Background paper on public assistance.
($3,049, original grant;
$11, refund)

Objective. To prepare an overview of the field of public assistance as related to urban problems; this involves the interface between human resource economics and the economics of public expenditures.

Results. A manuscript has been prepared and is now under review.

20 and 21. RESEARCH AT RESOURCES FOR THE FUTURE
A large portion of the CUE budget earmarked for employee compensation was in effect spent on research and related activities. This item includes the salaries of Wilbur Thompson and Irving Hoch while they were both employed

by Resources for the Future and served as ex-officio members of CUE. During his tenure, Thompson wrote *A Preface to Urban Economics.* Baltimore: The Johns Hopkins Press for Resources for the Future, 1965. The book is designed not only for scholars and administrators, but also for use as a textbook in upper-level classes. Thompson also directed the organization of the university matching grant program (see Appendix L). Hoch engaged in research resulting in "The Three-Dimensional City: Contained Urban Space," chapter 3 in *The Quality of the Urban Environment: Essays on "New Resources" in an Urban Age,* edited by Harvey S. Perloff. Baltimore: The Johns Hopkins Press for Resources for the Future, 1969. CUE funds were also allocated to the preparation of the present report.

Appendix I
CUE Communication Grants

A major CUE goal has been to improve the amount and quality of information in the field of urban economics. A number of CUE grants have had the purpose of surveying the field (or part of the field) or of setting up information services of use to scholars in the field. These grants have been classified under the collective heading of communication grants, and the seven grants involved are described briefly here. (An eighth communication grant was not utilized when the project involved was terminated and grant funds were returned.)

Individual Grant Information[1]

Communication grants are described in terms of institution receiving grant; person(s) involved; amount and date of grant; objective and results.

1. UNIVERSITY OF PENNSYLVANIA   (William L. C. Wheaton)
   $800 (1960)   Conference to develop metropolitan spatial-transportation models.

   Objective and Results. Meeting for development of metropolitan spatial-transportation models. Sponsored by Institute for Urban Studies of the University of Pennsylvania. The invited scholars considered problems in the projections of location of land use and economic activity.

2. JOINT CENTER FOR URBAN STUDIES OF THE
   MASSACHUSETTS INSTITUTE OF TECHNOLOGY
   AND HARVARD UNIVERSITY   (Helen Kistin)
   $5,000 (1960)   Report on data needs.

   Objective. To identify the data needs of researchers and scholars in urban economics. More specific questions addressed: (1) What kinds of materials should be collected and communicated to facilitate research? (2) What functions are served by communications devices? (3) What functions are served by centralized information storage and collection?

   Results. Helen Kistin. "Urban Economic Research: Improving the Accessibility and Utilization of Literature, Data and Data Sources." Cambridge: Joint Center for Urban Studies of the Massachusetts Institute of Technology and Harvard University, January 1961. (Mimeo.)

---

1. Financial summaries of these items appear in Appendix Table G-4 in slightly different order.

3. INDIANA UNIVERSITY, GRADUATE SCHOOL OF BUSINESS

(Arthur M. Weimer)

$1,500 (1962)   Conference on applied urban economics.

Objective. To bring together officials from schools of business administration associated with the Big Ten schools, leaders of the business community, and members of the Committee on Urban Economics to discuss the preparation of curricula in applied urban economics for business schools

Results. The conference was held as planned. Conference proceedings were published: Arthur M. Weimer. *Conference on Applied Urban Economics.* Indiana University School of Business, Bureau of Business Research: Indiana Readings in Business No. 40, 1962. (See also Appendix J.)

4. UNIVERSITY OF ILLINOIS   (Scott Keyes)
   a. $10,000 (1962)   Survey of urban and regional education and
      $300, supplemental (1963) research in American universities.
   b. $ 9,300 (1966)   Expansion and improvement of periodical
                                 entitled *Research Digest.*

Objective and Results of (a): To survey urban and regional research activities and educational programs at U.S. universities offering programs leading to the doctoral degree, and to develop a mechanism for keeping this survey up to date. This eventuated in: Scott Keyes. *Urban and Regional Studies at U.S. Universities.* Baltimore: The Johns Hopkins Press for Resources for the Future, 1964.

Objective and Results of (b): Since 1954, the Bureau of Community Planning of the University of Illinois has prepared and distributed the semiannual publication, *Research Digest,* which served as a medium of communication in the urban and regional field. The Bureau undertook to improve and expand the coverage and content of the *Research Digest,* with the support of CUE, the University of Illinois, and the National Science Foundation. This was carried out and the publication was expanded. In 1968, the Ford Foundation made a grant of $64,000 to the University of Illinois to begin publication of a *Quarterly Digest of Urban and Regional Research* reporting work in progress in the field. It replaced the semiannual *Research Digest,* with the issue of Fall 1968. The *Digest* now has 700 subscribers and publishes as many as 400 research abstracts per issue.

5. UNIVERSITY OF PENNSYLVANIA   (Britton Harris)
   $2,500 (1964)   Seminar on models of land use development.
   The grant was made
   and the seminar
   held, but grant funds
   were not utilized.

Objective. To survey the state of knowledge with regard to models of land use development through a two-day seminar of experts in the field.

Results. Seminar was held at the University of Pennsylvania on October 22-24, 1964. Papers appeared in a special issue of *Journal of the American Institute of Planners,* May 1965.

6. STANFORD UNIVERSITY, COMMITTEE ON URBAN
   PUBLIC ECONOMICS   (Julius Margolis)
   a. $ 4,250 (1965)   An analysis of research needs for the study of
                           cost functions of urban public services.
   b. $18,000 (1967)   Seminar meetings of Committee on Urban Pub-
                           lic Economics.

Objective and Results of (a): To survey the state of knowledge on the cost of urban public services. The grant was used to pay for the services (during one summer) of John Kain of Harvard University, who prepared a report which was the basis of a research seminar sponsored by the Committee on Urban Public Economics.

Objective and Results of (b): To provide some incentives and guides for research in state and local public economics through a research seminar, bringing together scholars with an interest in public finance problems. This was carried out through the 1967-68 seminar program of COUPE.

7. WASHINGTON UNIVERSITY   (Charles Leven, John Martinson)
   $12,000 (1966)   Information services in urban economics.

Objective. The increasing volume of research and materials in urban economics implies a need for specialized information activities to provide rapid access by scholars to news about important developments in the field and to research results as they accumulate.

Results. To meet this need, the following experimental publications were introduced: (1) *News in Urban Economics,* a newsletter; and (2) *Reviews in Urban Economics,* a semiannual collection of articles reviewing the literature in particular problem areas, prepared by graduate students working under the guidance of an interuniversity faculty committee. The publications were not successfully established as ongoing enterprises. However, the experience with them gave some evidence of general interest in publications of this kind.

Appendix J
CUE Conferences and Publications

CUE and its related advisory committees organized a number of conferences to further the development of urban economics. In many cases, conference proceedings were subsequently published under RFF auspices. A list of conferences and subsequent publications is presented below. Appendix M lists participants in the major conferences; the contents pages of the published proceedings conclude this appendix.

As noted in Appendix H, Wilbur Thompson's *A Preface to Urban Economics* was published by The Johns Hopkins Press for Resources for the Future, Inc.; CUE was the source of support for Thompson's work on the book.

Table J-1 shows publication experience on the conference proceedings and on Thompson's book.

List of Conferences and Subsequent Publications

Committee	Conference	Publication
Committee on Urban Human Resources	HR 1: Conference on the Economics of Human Resources (1961)	—
	HR 2: Conference on the Economics of Urban Human Resources (1962)	*Human Resources in the Urban Economy* —papers presented at a 1962 conference sponsored by the Committee on Urban Economics. Mark Perlman, ed. 1963.
Committee on Regional Accounts	RA 1: Conference on Regional Accounts (1960)	*Design of Regional Accounts*—papers presented at the Conference on Regional Accounts, 1960. Werner Hochwald, ed. 1961.
	RA 2: Second Conference on Regional Accounts (1962)	*Elements of Regional Accounts*—papers presented at the Conference on Regional Accounts, 1962, sponsored by the Committee on Regional Accounts. Werner Z. Hirsch, ed. 1964.
	RA 3: Third Conference on Regional Accounts (1964)	*Regional Accounts for Policy Decisions*—papers presented at the Conference on Regional Accounts, 1964, sponsored by the Committee on Regional Accounts. Werner Z. Hirsch, ed. 1966

	RA 4: Fourth Conference on Regional Accounts (1968)	—
Committee on Urban Public Expenditures	UPE 1: Conference on Public Expenditure Decisions in the Urban Community (1962)	*Public Expenditure Decisions in the Urban Community*—papers presented at a 1962 conference sponsored by the Committee on Urban Economics. Howard G. Schaller, ed. 1963.
	UPE 2: Second Conference on Urban Public Expenditures (1964)	*The Public Economy of Urban Communities*—papers presented at a 1964 conference sponsored by the Committee on Urban Economics. Julius Margolis, ed. 1965.
Committee on Urban Economics	UEC: Conference on Urban Economics: Analytical and Policy Issues (1967)	*Issues in Urban Economics:* Based on papers presented at a conference sponsored by the Committee on Urban Economics of RFF, Harvey S. Perloff and Lowdon Wingo, Jr., eds. 1968.
		Revenue Sharing and the City. Based on a conference sponsored by the Committee on Urban Economics. Walter W. Heller, Richard Ruggles, *et al.* Harvey S. Perloff and Richard P. Nathan, eds. 1968.

Other Conferences

Conference on Economics of Urban Migration (1960). New York. Co-sponsored with Institute of Public Administration. A two-day conference of economists, sociologists, and administrators concerned with population movements to and between cities.

CUE Seminar on Intra-Metropolitan Models (1961). A meeting of fourteen scholars from ten organizations, to discuss the current state and future needs of research in metropolitan spatial organization.

Applied Urban Economics Conference (1961). Co-sponsored with Graduate School of Business, Indiana University. Identification of major problem areas in the interrelationships between the business firm and the urban community. A meeting of business leaders and members of CUE.

Second Conference on Applied Urban Economics (1962). Co-sponsored with Graduate School of Business, Indiana University. A meeting of officials from schools of business administration associated with the Big Ten schools and members of the Committee on Urban Economics to discuss the preparation of curricula in applied urban economics for business schools. Leaders of the business community also participated to help focus the discussion on the kinds of problems in the field of urban economics they encounter in the decision making of their firms. Proceedings: *Conference on Applied Urban Economics.* Indiana Readings in Business No. 40. Indiana University, Bureau of Business Research, School of Business, 1962. 21 pp.

Table J-1. Publication Experience for CUE Materials

Volume	Binding	Date published	No. of copies printed	No. sold[a]	Total distribution[a]
Design of Regional Accounts (Hochwald, ed.)	cloth	Dec. 1961	2,188	1,962	2,150
Elements of Regional Accounts (Hirsch, ed.)	cloth	June 1964	2,500	1,749	1,946
Regional Accounts for Policy Decisions (Hirsch, ed.)	cloth	Aug. 1966	2,505	1,732	1,928
A Preface to Urban Economics (Thompson)[b]	cloth	July 1965 July 1967	} 13,000	8,016	8,439
	paper	March 1968 March 1969	} 14,805	5,738	6,054
Human Resources in the Urban Economy (Perlman, ed.)	paper	Jan. 1964 and Aug. 1964	2,524	1,756	2,185
Public Expenditure Decisions in the Urban Community (Schaller, ed.)	paper	Jan. 1964 and May 1965	3,531	2,432	2,830
The Public Economy of Urban Communities (Margolis, ed.)	paper	Dec. 1965 and Jan. 1969	4,003	2,145	2,484
Issues in Urban Economics (Perloff and Wingo, eds.)[b]	cloth	July 1968 and	4,531	1,870	2,033
	paper	March 1969	11,318	4,808	5,092
Revenue Sharing and the City (Heller et al.)	cloth	March 1968	1,995	1,159	1,255
	paper		4,026	2,981	3,015

[a] As of March 31, 1969.

[b] The Library of Urban Affairs selected Thompson, *A Preface to Urban Economics* and Perloff and Wingo, eds., *Issues in Urban Economics* to be monthly book selections. The approximately 2,000 copies of each volume taken by the Library for distribution are not included in the totals above. There are to be Japanese and Spanish editions of Thompson's book.

Design of
REGIONAL
ACCOUNTS

Papers presented at the
Conference on Regional Accounts, 1960
Sponsored by the
COMMITTEE ON REGIONAL ACCOUNTS

Edited by Werner Hochwald

PUBLISHED FOR RESOURCES FOR THE FUTURE, INC.
BY THE JOHNS HOPKINS PRESS, BALTIMORE

CONTENTS

ELEMENTS OF
REGIONAL ACCOUNTS

Papers presented
at the Conference on
Regional Accounts, 1962

Sponsored by the
COMMITTEE ON REGIONAL ACCOUNTS

Edited by
WERNER Z. HIRSCH

PUBLISHED FOR RESOURCES FOR THE FUTURE, INC.
By The Johns Hopkins Press, Baltimore

CONTENTS

ix

REGIONAL ACCOUNTS
for POLICY DECISIONS

Edited by
WERNER Z. HIRSCH

Sponsored by the Committee on Regional Accounts
By The Johns Hopkins Press, Baltimore

CONTENTS

The Public
Economy of
Urban Communities

Papers presented at the second
Conference on Urban Public Expenditures,
held February 21-22, 1964, under the
sponsorship of the Committee on Urban Economics
of Resources for the Future, Inc.

EDITED BY JULIUS MARGOLIS

RESOURCES FOR THE FUTURE, INC.
1755 Massachusetts Avenue, N.W., Washington, D.C. 20036

Distributed by
THE JOHNS HOPKINS PRESS
Baltimore, Maryland 21218

CONTENTS

Contents

PUBLIC EXPENDITURE DECISIONS
IN THE URBAN COMMUNITY

Papers presented at a conference,
May 14-15, 1962, under the sponsorship of
the Committee on Urban Economics of
Resources for the Future, Inc.

Edited by
Howard G. Schaller

(Rff)

Distributed by
The Johns Hopkins Press, Baltimore, Md. 21218

Resources for the Future, Inc.
1755 Massachusetts Avenue, N.W. Washington, D.C. 20036

Contents

CONTENTS

ISSUES
IN
URBAN
ECONOMICS

Based on Papers Presented at a Conference
Sponsored by the Committee on Urban Economics
of Resources for the Future, Inc.

Edited by *Harvey S. Perloff and Lowdon Wingo, Jr.*

Published for Resources for the Future, Inc.
by The Johns Hopkins Press

Appendix K
CUE Fellowship Program

The CUE fellowship program was initiated in December 1959, by announcement to fifty-five department chairmen and deans of the program's establishment. Each was invited to nominate one candidate, and the limitation of one departmental candidate per year was retained thereafter. Nominated candidates filed an application form and included an example of their scholarly writing. The fellowship award initially consisted of $3,500 plus tuition to cover an eleven-month program of full-time research applicable to the recipient's doctoral dissertation. The awards were based on: (1) an estimate of the ability of the applicant to produce a research product of scholarly quality, and (2) the significance of the proposed line of inquiry to the field of urban economics. The first fellowships were awarded in March 1960.

In mid-1960, the departmental basis of the grants was broadened to include fields outside economics and business administration. Eligibility was extended to students in geography, political science, public administration, regional science, sociology, and urban planning, given an adequate grounding in graduate economics and a thesis topic germane to urban economics.

In 1962, the stipend was related to family status, with a nine-month term and a possible two-month extension. The total award consisted of tuition plus $2,500 if single or married with no children; $3,400 if married with one child; and $3,700 if married with two children. If a two-month extension was approved, the stipend was increased by two-ninths of the original amount. By 1962, award information was made available to ninety-six departments and schools. The final CUE fellowship grants were awarded in 1967.

Fellowship information on an annual basis is presented in Table K-1. A total of thirty-nine fellowships were awarded over the period 1960-67. In 1968, the corresponding doctorate experience was twenty-five doctorates awarded, three discontinued, and eleven in process. A check with university departments in late 1968 yielded evaluations of good progress for seven of the eleven, with completion anticipated within the coming year.

In addition, an attempt was made to contact the twenty-five successful candidates regarding their postdoctoral experience, and information was obtained from twenty of them. At least some of the current work of seventeen of the twenty is in urban economics. Seven persons worked full-time and twelve persons spent at least half their work time in the field. The average of time devoted to the field was 58 per cent for the group of twenty.

The twenty respondents indicated extensive publication of materials based on their dissertations; i.e., as of 1968, three books had been published or

Table K-1. CUE Fellowship Information (as of 1968)

Year	Number of fellowships awarded	Results		
		Doctorate awarded	Discon-tinued	In process (presumed)
1960	3	2	1	0
1961	7	6	1[a]	0
1962	5	3	0	2
1963	3	3	0	0
1964	5	4	1[b]	0
1965	6	4	0	2
1966	3	2	0	1
1967	7	1	0	6
Total	39	25	3	11
Total 1960-64	23	18	3	2

[a] Fellow deceased.

[b] Fellow changed to doctoral program in college administration; obtained Ph.D. in that field.

accepted for publication and three books were planned; forty-two articles, monographs, or reports had been published or accepted for publication and at least eight more submitted or planned. (Of the forty-two published items in the latter category, fifteen had been produced by one quite prolific scholar.)

A list of individual fellowship recipients follows; the list also includes respective school, discipline, dissertation title, status of doctoral work, and last known location. Three tables conclude this appendix. The distributions of fellowships by discipline and by university are presented in Tables K-2 and K-3, respectively. Table K-4 presents information on postdoctoral experience for the twenty CUE fellows from whom such information was obtained.

Urban Economics Fellowships

Fellowship recipients by year. Name of Fellow; university; discipline; thesis title; disposition of work; last known location of Fellow, by date.

1960

BRIAN W. BROGAN. The Johns Hopkins University. Economics. "Location theory and urban growth." Discontinued. Faculty of economics and statistics, Monash University, Clayton, Victoria, Australia (1965).

JAMES HEILBRUN. Columbia University. Economics. "The effects of alternative real estate tax systems on the maintenance and rehabilitation of urban rental housing." Ph.D. awarded 1964. Assistant Professor of Economics, Columbia University (1968).

RICHARD D. RAYMOND. Brown University. Economics. "Interaction between discrimination, interregional migration and regional development." Ph.D. awarded 1963. Assistant Professor of Economics, West Virginia University (1968).

104

GEORGE W. BLEILE. Northwestern University. Economics. "A theory of suburbanization of manufacturing activity." Fellow deceased.

DONALD J. CURRAN. University of Wisconsin. Economics. "The financial evolution of the Milwaukee Metropolitan Area." Ph.D. awarded 1963. Research Associate, Cambridge Center for Social Studies, Cambridge,. Massachusetts (1968).

ARNOLD M. FADEN. Columbia University. Economics. "Essays in spatial economics." Ph.D. awarded 1967. Assistant Professor, Department of Economics, Iowa State University (1968).

MAHFUZUL HUQ. Washington University. Economics. "Urban government service accounts." Ph.D. awarded 1963. Lecturer, Faculty of Economic and Social Studies, University of Khartoum, Sudan (1965).

WILLIAM C. PENDLETON. University of Chicago. Economics. "The value of highway accessibility." Ph.D. awarded 1963. Program Officer, Urban and Metropolitan Development, The Ford Foundation (1968).

HERMAN PORTER. Northwestern University. Geography. "Application of intercity intervening opportunity models to telephone, migration and highway traffic data." Ph.D. awarded 1964. Computer Programmer, Computer Applications, Inc., New York City (1965).

THOMAS A. REINER. University of Pennsylvania. Regional Science. "Regional allocation criteria." Ph.D. awarded 1963. Associate Professor, Regional Science Department, University of Pennsylvania (1968).

1962

WILLIAM CHAULK BIRDSALL. The Johns Hopkins University. Economics. "Public finance allocation decisions and the preferences of citizens: some theoretical and empirical considerations." Ph.D. awarded 1963. Economist, Long Range Planning Branch, Office of Research and Statistics, Social Security Administration, Washington, D.C. (1967).

STANISLAW CZAMANSKI. University of Pennsylvania. Regional Science. "A model of urban growth." Ph.D. awarded 1963. Associate Professor of Regional Planning, Cornell University (1968).

JOHN C. HAGGART. University of California, Los Angeles. Business Administration. "Authority in municipal organizations for the integration of urban renewal plans." Ph.D. awarded 1963. Associate Professor of Management, Loyola University of Los Angeles (1967).

EDWARD E. LAITILA. Indiana University. Business Administration. "An economic evaluation of area redevelopment administration assistance in selected counties of Southern Illinois and Northern Michigan." Not completed. Economist, Battelle Memorial Institute, Columbus, Ohio (1967).

JANET SCHEFF REINER. University of Pennsylvania. City Planning. "Evaluation and determination of public policy through client analysis." Not completed. Consultant, University of Puerto Rico, Graduate Program in Planning; University of Pennsylvania, Fels Institute of Local and State Government and Institute for Environmental Studies (1967).

1963

FREDERICK W. BELL. Wayne State University. Economics. "The elasticity of substitution, wage differentials and structural unemployment in urban economies." Ph.D. awarded 1964. Chief, Branch of Economics Research, U.S. Bureau of Commercial Fisheries, U.S. Department of the Interior, Washington, D.C. (1968).

WARREN F. MAZEK. University of Pittsburgh. Economics. "The efficacy of labor migration with special emphasis on depressed areas." Ph.D. awarded 1965. Assistant Professor of Economics, Florida State University (1968).

SAMUEL L. THORNDIKE, JR. Columbia University. Economics. "Problems in appraising the economic impact of a transportation improvement: A theoretical exploration." Ph.D. awarded 1967. Assistant Professor of Economics, University of Wisconsin, Milwaukee (1968).

1964

JAY STARRETT BERGER. University of California, Los Angeles. Business Administration. "Determination of the economic height of high-rise buildings." Ph.D. awarded 1967. Assistant Professor of Finance and Real Estate, San Fernando Valley State College (1968).

DONALD GERWIN. Carnegie Institute of Technology. Industrial Administration. "A process model of budgeting in public administration." Ph.D. awarded 1967. Assistant Professor, School of Business Administration, University of Wisconsin, Milwaukee, Wisconsin (1968).

WILLIAM R. MANN. Yale University. Economics. "Optimizing government expenditures on juvenile delinquency." Discontinued. Changed to doctoral program in college administration. Obtained Ph.D. at the University of Michigan. Assistant Dean of Academic Affairs, Kalamazoo College, Kalamazoo, Michigan (1968).

JERRY B. SCHNEIDER. University of Pennsylvania. Regional Science. "Planning the growth of a metropolitan system of public-service facilities: the case of the short-term general hospital." Ph.D. awarded 1966. Staff Director, Seattle Office, Regional Science Research Institute, Seattle, Washington (1968).

JOHN CHARLES WEICHER. University of Chicago. Economics. "The effect of urban renewal on the cost of municipal government services." Ph.D. awarded 1968. Assistant Professor of Economics, The Ohio State University, Columbus, Ohio (1968).

1965

EUGENE J. DEVINE. University of California, Los Angeles. Economics. "Manpower shortages in local government employment." Not completed. Instructor, Simon Fraser University, Burnaby, British Columbia, Canada (1967).

JOHN D. HEINBERG. University of Wisconsin, Madison. Economics. "Public policy toward residential rehabilitation: an economic analysis." Ph.D. awarded

1967. Assistant Professor of Economics and Public Affairs, Princeton University, Princeton, New Jersey (1968).

WALTER P. HETTICH. Yale University. Economics. "Equalization grants, minimum standards, and unit cost differences in education." Ph.D. awarded 1967. Assistant Professor of Economics, Queen's University, Kingston, Ontario, Canada (1968).

THOMAS E. LISCO. University of Chicago. Economics. "The value of commuters' travel time: A study in urban transportation." Ph.D. awarded 1967. Research Associate, Chicago Area Transportation Study, Chicago, Illinois (1968).

ROBERT G. McGILLIVRAY. University of California, Berkeley. Economics. "The demand for urban travel and residential space." Not completed. Instructor and Graduate Student, Department of Economics, University of California, Berkeley, California (1967).

PHAICHITR UATHAVIKUL. Cornell University. Regional Planning. "Decision theory and regional economic growth: A model of resource utilization in the context of regional opportunity loss." Ph.D. awarded 1966. Acting Dean, School of Development Economics, National Institute of Development Administration, Bangkok, Thailand (1967).

1966

RICHARD D. ERB. Stanford University. Economics. "An economic analysis of urban residential blight." Ph.D. awarded 1968. Board of Governors of the Federal Reserve System (1968).

FRANK S. LEVY. Yale University. Economics. "Two essays on the Racial Imbalance Act of Massachusetts." In process. Assistant Professor, Department of Economics, University of California, Berkeley (1967).

LARRY L. ORR. Massachusetts Institute of Technology. Economics. "Municipal governmental policy and the location of population and industry in a metropolitan area: an econometric study." Ph.D. awarded 1967. Assistant Professor of Economics, University of Wisconsin, Madison (1968).

1967

JAMES C. COX. Harvard University. Economics. "Simulation of the elimination of poverty in the Boston Metropolitan Area." In process. Graduate Student, Harvard University (1967).

BRYAN C. ELLICKSON. Massachusetts Institute of Technology. Economics. "Transportation and urban structure." In process. Assistant Professor, Department of Economics, University of California, Los Angeles (1968).

JOHN L. GARDNER. University of Minnesota. Economics. "Occupational differentials in the propensity to migrate." In process. Graduate Student, University of Minnesota (1967).

DAVID S. SHAPIRA. Stanford University. Economics. "Urban renewal: its effects on city financial resources." In process. Graduate Student, Stanford University (1967).

DONALD C. SHOUP. Yale. Economics. "Advance land acquisition by local governments: A cost-benefit analysis." Ph.D. awarded 1968. Institute of Government and Public Affairs, University of California, Los Angeles (1968).

IRVING R. SILVER. Massachusetts Institute of Technology. City and Regional Planning. "A model of the metropolitan housing market." In process. Graduate Student, Massachusetts Institute of Technology (1967).

NICOLAUS T. TIDEMAN. University of Chicago. Economics. "The economics of urban land control." In process. Assistant Professor, Department of Economics, Harvard University (1968).

Table K-2. Distribution of CUE Fellowships by Discipline

Discipline	Number of fellowships
Economics	28
Business administration	3
Industrial administration	1
Regional science	3
City and regional planning	3
Geography	1
Total	39

Table K-3. Distribution of CUE Fellowships by University

University	Number of CUE fellowships
Brown University	1
Carnegie Institute of Technology	1
University of California, Berkeley	1
University of California, Los Angeles	3
University of Chicago	4
Columbia University	3
Cornell University	1
Harvard University	1
Indiana University	1
Johns Hopkins University	2
Massachusetts Institute of Technology	3
University of Minnesota	1
Northwestern University	2
University of Pennsylvania	4
University of Pittsburgh	1
Stanford University	2
Washington University, St. Louis	1
Wayne State University	1
University of Wisconsin	2
Yale University	4
Total	39

Table K-4. Postdoctoral Experience of Twenty CUE Fellows (as of 1968)

Fellow	Estimate of percentage of current work in urban economics	Publications based on thesis
Frederick W. Bell	0	"A Note on the Empirical Estimation of the CES Production Function with the Use of Capital Data." *The Review of Economics and Statistics* (August 1965). "The Role of Capital-Labor Substitution in the Economic Adjustment of an Industry across Regions." *The Southern Economic Journal* XXXI (October 1964).
Jay Berger	50	Monograph: *The Determination of the Economic Height of High-Rise Buildings.* Occasional Paper No. 3. Housing, Real Estate and Urban Land Studies Program, Graduate School of Business Administration. Los Angeles: University of California, May 1968.
William C. Birdsall	Not given	Section of book: "A Study of the Demand for Public Goods," in *Essays in Fiscal Federalism*, edited by Richard A. Musgrave. Washington, D. C.: Brookings Institution, 1965.
Donald J. Curran	25	Four articles published: possible publication as a book being considered. Articles: "The Metropolitan Problem: Solution From Within?" *National Tax Journal* XVI (September 1963), pp. 213-33. "Intra-Metropolitan Competition." *Land Economics* XL (February 1964), pp. 94-99. "Historical Approach to a Study of a Metropolitan Area." *Land Economics* XLII (May 1966), pp. 209-15. "Social Change and Political Lag in Metropolitan Milwaukee." *The American Journal of Economics and Sociology* 25 (July 1966), pp. 229-42.
Stanislaw Czamanski	100	Three articles published: "A Model of Urban Growth." *Papers and Proceedings, Regional Science Association* XIII (1965). "Industrial Location and Urban Growth," *The Town Planning Review*, Liverpool, 36 (October 1965). "A Method of Forecasting Metropolitan Growth by Means of Distributed Lags Analysis." *Journal of Regional Science* VI, No. 1 (1965).

Table K-4. (*Continued*)

Fellow	Estimate of percentage of current work in urban economics	Publications based on thesis
Arnold Faden	30	Article: "Industrial Location on the Euclidean Plane." *Geographical Analysis* 1 (January 1969). Book in process for the Johns Hopkins Press: *Foundations of Spatial Economics*.
Donald Gerwin	25	Entire study to be published by the University of Wisconsin Press in 1969. Tentative title: "Budgetary Decisions in the Public Sector: A Simulation Study of an Urban School District." A review of the work has been accepted by *Management Science* subject to final revision: "A Process Model of Budgeting in a Public School System." One aspect of the study appears in "Compensation Decisions in Public Organizations," *Industrial Relations*, February 1969. Another article has been submitted for publication.
James Heilbrun	60	Book: *Real Estate Taxes and Urban Housing*. New York: Columbia University Press, 1966.
John D. Heinberg	100	Thesis under consideration for publication in book form.
Walter Hettich	30	Condensed version of thesis appears in *Yale Economic Essays* under title "Equalization Grants, Minimum Standards, and Unit Cost Differences in Education," Fall 1968, pp. 5-55.
Thomas E. Lisco	100	Paper presented at Highway Research Board meetings, January 1968. Abstract appears in *Highway Research Record* 245, p. 36, under the title "Value of Commuters' Travel Time—A Study in Urban Transportation." A book is planned.
Warren Mazek	20	*The Efficacy of Labor Migration with Special Emphasis on Depressed Areas*. Working Paper No. 2, Institute for Urban and Regional Studies. St. Louis, Washington University, 1966. This is a slightly modified version of the dissertation. "Unemployment and Migration: The Case of Laborers." *Journal of Regional Science* 9 (April 1969).
Larry L. Orr	50	Dissertation tentatively accepted (subject to revisions) for publication as a monograph by the Harvard-M.I.T. Joint Center for Urban Studies. Article: "The Incidence of Differential Property Taxes on Urban Housing." *National Tax Journal* (September 1968).

Name	%	Publications
William Pendleton	100	"The Use of Statistical Inference in Appraisal and Assessment Procedures." *The Appraisal Journal* (January 1965); and "Relation of Highway Accessibility to Urban Real Estate Values." *Highway Research Record* 16 (1963).
Richard Raymond	0	One article submitted for publication, three others planned.
Thomas A. Reiner	40	Publications which are essentially chapters from the dissertation: "Regional and National Economic Planning, and Analytic Techniques for Implementation," Chapter 1 in: *Regional Economic Planning*, edited by Walter Isard and John H. Cumberland. Paris: European Productivity Agency, 1961 (with Walter Isard). "A Choice Theory of Planning." *Journal of the American Institute of Planners* XXVIII (May 1962). "Organizing Regional Investment Criteria." *Papers, The Regional Science Association* XI (1963). "Sub-National and National Planning; Decision Criteria." *Papers, The Regional Science Association* XIV (1965). "Spatial Criteria to Offset Military Cutbacks." *Papers, Peace Research Society (International)* III (1965). Ten other articles related to the dissertation have been published.
Jerry B. Schneider	100	"Measuring the Locational Efficiency of the Urban Hospital." *Health Services Research* 2 (Summer 1967), pp. 154-69. "A New Approach to Areawide Planning of Metropolitan Hospital Systems." *Hospitals, Journal of the American Hospital Association* 42 (April 16, 1968), pp. 79-83. "Measuring, Evaluating and Redesigning Hospital-Physician-Patient Spatial Relationships in Metropolitan Areas," *Inquiry* V (June 1968), pp. 24-43.
Donald Shoup	100	Much of material to be published as a HUD monograph: *Advance Land Acquisition by Local Governments*. A reduced version of the thesis is expected to appear in the *Yale Economic Essays*.
Samuel L. Thorndike	80	Some sections may be submitted for publication as articles.
John C. Weicher	100	Two articles under preparation for possible publication.

Appendix L
CUE Matching Grants to Universities

The activities of CUE in the first grant period had an exploratory focus; in the second grant period, there was a shift in emphasis to promoting expansion of the educational and research base in urban economics. Basic education needs seen at the start of the second grant period were: (1) introductory courses in urban economics, (2) graduate seminars and workshops, and (3) postdoctoral fellowships. On this last item, the second grant proposal noted the need for a fellowship that would "purchase part of a young scholar's time during the two years immediately following his Ph.D. award for free research along lines suggested by his dissertation."

By early 1965, the Committee had concluded that systematic action to strengthen university programs was needed to accomplish these ends. The case for such action included the argument that the programs would continue after the completion of the CUE grant, which was a terminal grant. The specific approach adopted was a system of matching grants, which contained the following elements:

1. The Committee would contribute $75,000 to a university to support a program in urban economics, if this were matched by a university grant of $125,000. The initial arrangement proposed was an annual grant by CUE of $25,000 for three years, with an annual university grant at the same level for five years. (In practice, however, the CUE grant for some programs was set at $15,000 annually over a five-year period.) It was hoped that at the end of the five-year period, the urban economics program would have proved its worth, and thereafter it would be funded on a permanent basis by the university.
2. The participating university's contribution would be earmarked as research funds for research assistants, data collection, computer costs, travel expenses, secretarial help, and similar direct research operating costs, and would not be used for staffing or reducing teaching loads.
3. The participating university would offer a curriculum in urban economics or regional economics (with a strong urban content) as a field of specialization in its doctoral program.
4. The participating university would have under way or imminent a research program in urban economics that could serve as an extension of predoctoral and postdoctoral education programs.

The Committee further agreed that it would be desirable to promote some exchange of personnel among the various university programs supported by CUE, and that some co-ordination of research programs would help develop an effective consortium of centers of education and research in urban economics.

Letters describing the matching grant program were sent to university departments that seemed potentially interested and able to meet the grant conditions. Those responding favorably were invited to submit a detailed application for a matching grant.

The following criteria were specified for choosing the departments to receive grants:

1. The university would give firm assurance of its commitment to support education and research in urban economics up to and beyond expiration of the grant period.
2. Several people in the department would be committed to the field so that it would have some depth and the program would not be discontinued if one person should leave after it was instituted.
3. The university would grant a Ph.D. degree in economics or business administration with a specialty in urban economics; that is, a student could take urban economics as his major field in working towards a Ph.D.
4. The program in urban economics would be strongly backed by work in urban affairs carried by other disciplines and schools, including sociology, political science, geography, city planning, etc.
5. The proposal would meet the requirements outlined in the letter that was sent to the interested university departments, including a commitment of five years of university financing.

Of the departments making applications, only five met all the conditions of the program; full matching grants were made to the respective universities in 1966. These "major grant" departments, and their corresponding grants, were:

University of California, Los Angeles (economics)	
Washington University, St. Louis (economics)	Three annual grants of $25,000 each.
Indiana University (business school)	
Wayne State University (economics)	Five annual grants of $15,000 each.
Syracuse University (economics)	

Over the next two years, additional matching grants were made to five universities that did not fully meet all the grant conditions but had activities in the field promising enough to merit support. Because they were, in effect, at an earlier stage of development, the departments in this group were termed "pilot grant" departments. These departments, their grants, and the grant periods were:

Brown University (economics)	$25,000	July 1967-June 1969
University of Chicago (economics)	$45,000	May 1968-April 1973
Iowa State University (economics)	$15,000	June 1966-Aug. 1969
New York University (public administration[1])	$22,500	Sept. 1966-Aug. 1969
University of Pittsburgh (economics)	$26,750	Sept. 1967-Aug. 1970

1. The CUE grant was a joint grant to the Graduate School of Public Administration and the Graduate School of Business Administration. The urban economics program,

Table L-1. Educational Experience of CUE-Supported Programs: Number of Persons in Postdoctoral, Doctoral, and Predoctoral Programs (aggregate data, as of summer 1968)

Category	Five major grant departments[a]	Five pilot grant departments[b]	Ten-department total
Postdoctoral			
Postdoctoral Fellows	18	2	20
(CUE-supported)[c]	(17)	(0)	(17)
Doctoral			
Completed doctorates (1963-68)	25	10	35
(CUE-supported)[d]	(9)	(5)	(14)
Doctorates in progress	28	22	50
(CUE-supported)[d]	(16)	(9)	(25)
Total doctorates	53	32	85
(CUE-supported)[d]	(25)	(14)	(39)
Predoctoral (precandidacy students expected to present urban economics as a field for doctorate)			
Economics and business administration	57	37	94
All other	19	10	29
Total	76	47	123

[a] University of California, Los Angeles (economics); Indiana University (business school); Syracuse University (economics); Washington University, St. Louis (economics); Wayne State University (economics).

[b] Brown University (economics); University of Chicago (economics); Iowa State University (economics); New York University (public administration); University of Pittsburgh (economics).

[c] One Fellow (at Syracuse) received part of his support from a non-CUE source.

[d] Includes all persons receiving *some* CUE support through CUE fellowships and/or through university grants using CUE matching-grant funds.

The university contribution consisted of an equal amount in the cases of Brown University, Iowa State University, and the University of Pittsburgh; New York University agreed to contribute "at least an equal amount"; and the University of Chicago allotted $75,000 as its matching contribution.

Recent educational experience for departments receiving CUE grants is summarized in Table L-1 and presented in more detail in Table L-2. In both tables, doctoral support includes matching grant support and direct fellowship support (CUE fellowships as described in Appendix K).

For the ten departments as a group, almost all the postdoctoral fellowships were financed by CUE funds, as were roughly half of the doctorates. Thirty-five doctorates were completed over the last five years, and fifty were in progress as of summer 1968. As of that date approximately 125 precandidacy students were expected to present urban economics as a field for the doctorate; of these, roughly 100 were in economics and business administration. It seems

however, is administered by economists housed in public administration. In previous tables, the program has been classified under economics for ease of exposition. (See Table C-1, footnote b.)

Table L-2. Educational Experience of CUE-Supported Programs: Persons in Postdoctoral, Doctoral, and Predoctoral Programs (Individual university departments, as of summer 1968)

Category	U. of California, Los Angeles	Indiana U.	Syracuse U.	Washington U., St. Louis	Wayne State U.	Brown U.	U. of Chicago	Iowa State U.	New York U.	U. of Pittsburgh
Postdoctoral Fellows (1967-68)										
CUE-supported	2 (2)	9 (8)	3 (3)	2 (2)	2 (2)	0 (0)	1 (0)	0 (0)	0 (0)	1 (0)
Total fellow-years	3	6-1/3	3	3-1/2	1-1/2	0	1	0	0	1
Completed doctorates in urban economics (1963-68)	0	10	8	2	5	1	3	1	0	5
CUE-supported										
Matching grant	(0)	(4)	(0)	(0)	(3)	(0)	(0)	(0)	(0)	(0)
Direct	(0)	(0)	(0)	(1)	(1)	(1)	(3)	(0)	(0)	(1)
Doctorates in progress in urban economics	3	6	6	8	5	2	10	5	3	2
CUE-supported										
Matching grant	(1)	(4)	(2)	(2)	(5)	(2)	(2)	(2)	(0)	(2)
Direct	(1)	(1)	(0)	(0)	(0)	(0)	(1)	(0)	(0)	(0)
Precandidacy students expected to present urban economics as a field for doctorate										
Economics	10	7	10	13	12	5	5-10	4	<5	8
Business administration	a	5	–	0	0	–	5-10	–	<5	–
Other	a	8	10	1	0	–	–	–	5-10	3
Total	10+	20	20	14	12	5	15	4	12	11

a No specific number estimated, but a few students expected.

Table L-3. Courses and Enrollment in Urban Economics at Matching Grant Departments

Department	Number of courses in urban economics (1968)			Total course enrollment per year (average 1967-68)		
	Undergraduate credit only	Graduate credit	Total	Undergraduate credit only	Graduate credit	Total
Major grant departments						
University of California,						
Los Angeles (economics)	3	4	7	80	50	130
Indiana University (business school)	1	5	6	40	120	160
Syracuse University (economics)	2	6	8	65	195	260
Washington University (economics)	–	6	6	–	60	60
Wayne State University (economics)	–	5	5	–	100	100
Pilot grant departments						
Brown University (economics)	–	3	3	–	15	15
University of Chicago (economics)	–	6[a]	6[a]	–	125	125
Iowa State University (economics)	2	6	8	40	25	65
New York University						
(public administration)	1	6	7	35	125	160
University of Pittsburgh (economics)	–	6	6	–	125	125
Total: 5 major grant departments	6	26	32	185	525	710
Total: 5 pilot grant departments[a]	3	27	30	75	415	490
Grand total	9	53	62	260	940	1,200

[a] Two of the courses are somewhat marginal to the field, being centered in other programs in economics.

clear that these ten departments will be producing a substantial number of professional workers in the field of urban economics.

The major grant departments have awarded eighteen postdoctoral fellowships, as compared to two awarded by the pilot grant departments. Among the major grant departments, the business school at the Indiana University has put the most emphasis on the fellowship program, with nine postdoctoral fellowships versus two or three awarded by each of the other schools. Many of the Indiana awards were for summer terms, but a considerable differential remains when the comparison is on a full-time equivalent basis.

The major grant departments led the pilot grant departments in the number of doctorates completed over the period 1963-68 (twenty-five versus ten) as well as in doctorates in progress as of 1968 (twenty-eight versus twenty-two). The narrowing of the difference in totals between the two groups primarily reflects changes that occurred at the University of Chicago, Iowa State University, and New York University; at each, the number of doctorates in progress was well above the number of doctorates completed.

The number of precandidacy students at the major grant departments averaged about fifteen; at the pilot grant departments, the average was about ten. If these figures are good indicators of future doctorates, then Indiana University, Syracuse University, the University of Chicago, and Washington University should have the greatest number of doctorates initiated in the near future.

Table L-3 summarizes data on course work and enrollment in courses in the field for the matching grant departments. (A student enrolling in two courses is counted twice, etc.) In 1968, the five major grant departments had a total of thirty-two courses and an annual enrollment of 710. The pilot grant departments had thirty courses and an annual enrollment of 490. Hence, student enrollments in courses in the field totaled 1,200 per year for the ten university departments.

Table L-4. Dates of Introduction of Courses in Urban Economics at Matching Grant Departments   (Number of courses)

Year	Five major grant departments	Five pilot grant departments	Ten-department total
1968	0	0	0
1967	1	6	7
1966	12	6	18
1965	2	2	4
1964	0	5	5
1963	0	3	3
1962	4	1	5
1961	0	1	1
1960	1	0	1
1959	2	0	2
Pre-1959	1	0	1
Not listed	9	6	15
Total	32	30	62

Table L-4 lists the distribution of courses in urban economics by date of introduction. The impact of the CUE matching grants seems evident in the large number of courses introduced in 1966, particularly by the five major grant departments.

The remainder of this appendix is devoted to a short description of some of the high points of each of the matching grant programs.

High Points of Matching Grant Programs

Individual programs are described in the following order: faculty devoting half or more of teaching load to instruction in urban economics; other faculty; institutional organization of urban economics center; some program highlights; university evaluation of CUE support.

UNIVERSITY OF CALIFORNIA, LOS ANGELES (economics)
Major faculty (Faculty devoting half or more of teaching load to instruction in urban economics)

> Werner Z. Hirsch
> Bryan Ellickson

Other faculty

> Marvin Hoffenberg
> Donald Shoup
> Harold Somers
> Phillip Vincent
> Leland Burns (business school)

Institutional organization
Program administered by department of economics in collaboration with the Institute of Government and Public Affairs.

Program highlights

First Year
Graduate Workshop organized for spring semester, 1966. Topic: "Application of Benefit-Cost Analysis to Urban Decisions." Presented again 1966-67. Topic: "Urban Public Activities." Eight papers presented by students.

Martin Katzman, postdoctoral fellow 1966-67. Served as faculty member of graduate seminar on urban economics. Presented a COUPE paper. Submitted five papers for publication.

Eugene Devine and Morton Marcus prepared a paper for the *Western Economic Journal*, 1967. This received the 1967 Eliot Jones award of the Western Economics Association.

Hirsch prepared three papers, Martin Katzman prepared two parts for workshop presentation.

Second Year
Graduate Workshop topic: "Analysis of Urban Goals and Decisions."
Phillip Vincent, postdoctoral Fellow 1967-68. Served as faculty member of

the graduate seminar on urban economics. Submitted one paper for publication.

R. Teeples prepared a paper on "Some Problems Concerning the Magnitude of State and Local Government Revenues from User Charges."

Eugene Devine accepted an invitation to give a paper based on his dissertation in the special "dissertations sessions" at the December 1968 meetings of the American Economic Association.

Five persons received some CUE fellowship support.

Faculty research projects: regional information design; local government program budgeting (emphasis on welfare, education, police, and recreation); the economics of state and local government.

Outside related activities: faculty co-operative work with the City of Compton, the Los Angeles City Council, and the State of California.

University evaluation of CUE support
"The matching grant has provided additional stimulus to the urban economics program."

INDIANA UNIVERSITY (business school)
Major faculty
>Jerome W. Milliman (full-time)
>Richard L. Pfister (full-time)

Institutional organization
Training in urban economics is carried out in the Institute for Applied Urban Economics in the Graduate School of Business, co-operatively with the Department of Economics.

Program highlights
November 1965-August 1966
Richard L. Pfister joined faculty as Professor of Applied Urban Economics.
New courses established at both MBA and doctoral levels.
Postgraduate workshop established, summer 1966.
Publications arising out of workshop:
>Gilbert Churchill, article, *Southern Economic Journal.*
>Stephen D. Messner, monograph, Bureau of Business Research, Indiana University.
>John Munro, article submitted to *Land Economics.*
>Richard T. Pratt, articles, *Economic Geography* and *Journal of Regional Science.*

September 1966-August 1967
Each of Indiana's four postdoctoral fellows appeared on the program of the annual meetings of the Regional Science Association.
First graduate-faculty workshop established in applied urban economics.
Milliman served as consultant to Carnegie-Mellon University on the establishment of a new school of urban affairs.

September 1967-August 1968
Enrollment increases in all courses in urban economics.
Thirteen workshop sessions, with eight presentations by graduate students

or postdoctoral fellows (several were half sessions), and nine by outside scholars. The latter included: Otto Davis, Anthony Downs, Charles Leven, Bernard Booms, William Neenan, W. Lee Hansen, Joseph Persky, James Prescott, and Harold Rose. Workshop attendance ranged from twenty-one to forty-six. Attendance was especially heavy from throughout the University for the Downs, Persky, and Rose sessions dealing with American ghetto problems and policies.

Bernard Booms was appointed as a post-doctoral fellow beginning September 1, 1968.

Published articles and/or monographs were produced by Bish, Boehme, Brown, Churchill, Greytak, Mann, Messner, Munro, Nicholls, Olsen, and Pratt.

Milliman paper, "Urban Economic Developments and Water Resources Research" presented at Conference on Metropolitan Water Resources Research, April 17, 1968, Washington, D. C.

Pfister completed a study for the Indiana State Tax Commission entitled "An Analysis of Variations in Per Capita Expenditures of Indiana Cities for Selected Governmental Functions."

Some faculty research topics: theory of regional and urban growth; costs of urban services; urban water supply.

University evaluation of CUE support
"Without CUE funds we would have a very small program."

SYRACUSE UNIVERSITY (Economics, Maxwell Graduate School, Metropolitan Studies Program)
Major faculty
> Seymour Sacks (economics)
> Jesse Burkhead (economics)
> David Miller (economics)
> Gerald Karaska (geography)
> Alan K. Campbell (political science)

Other faculty
> J. Miner

Institutional organization
The Maxwell School's Metropolitan Studies Program is both an academic and research program. Students in the program may take an interdisciplinary doctorate or a regular Ph.D. in one of the departments (Economics, Geography, Political Science, Sociology).

Program highlights
First Year
David Miller joined the faculty in fall 1966; he introduced a graduate course in location theory.

An undergraduate course in urban economics was offered for the first time. It was taught by Herbert Werner, postdoctoral fellow. Werner later accepted a faculty position in economics, University of Missouri, St. Louis.

Progress was made in the development of an urban data bank, under Seymour Sacks. A substantial portion of the time of three research assistants was devoted to the project.

Several conferences were held.

Second Year

Undergraduate course offered again by Roy Bahl, postdoctoral fellow.

Bahl carried on an extensive program of research and publication. He later accepted a position with the International Monetary Fund. His publications included articles in *Land Economics, Journal of Regional Science,* and *Proceedings of the National Tax Association* and a monograph, *The Structure of Metropolitan Core City Expenditures,* University of Kentucky Press.

The urban economic data bank was expanded. It covers all 212 Standard Metropolitan Statistical Areas.

The data bank, per se is available on computer cards and tape; data bank printouts are also available, as is an *Introduction and Guide* to the data bank.

Burkhead and Campbell offered the Metropolitan Studies Seminar.

A special issue of *The Maxwell Review* (graduate student publication) was devoted to metropolitan studies, October 1967.

Faculty research topics include: urban land and property value models; ethnic aspects of urban housing; finances and policy-making in large city education; supply functions for urban mass transit; urbanization in British towns.

Burkhead directed research in urban educational finance; Campbell and Sacks published *Metropolitan America: Fiscal Patterns and Governmental Systems* in 1967.

Visiting lecturers included: Paul Spreiregen, architect, National Foundation on Arts and Humanities; Robert Simon, former director, Reston, Virginia; Jason Nathan, Housing and Development Administrator, New York City.

Faculty members have served as consultants to a number of state and local agencies.

University evaluation of CUE support

"The CUE grant has contributed importantly to the strengthening of the program in urban and regional economics. The fellowships have enabled us to attract good first-year students and have encouraged advanced graduate students to make this their field of specialization. The postdoctoral fellows have had responsibility for offering a new undergraduate one-semester course in urban economics. This will be a continuous departmental offering. In general, the grant has helped make our program visible, both on campus and nationally."

WASHINGTON UNIVERSITY (economics)
Major faculty

        Charles L. Leven
        John B. Legler
        Richard F. Muth

Other faculty

        Harold Barnett
        Jack Triplett
        Murray Weidenbaum

Institutional organization

Education in urban economics is administered by the department of economics and research by the Institute for Urban and Regional Studies.

Program

The Institute for Urban and Regional Studies was reorganized and reactivated in fall 1965.

Research projects:

"Design of Regional Account System," financed by CUE (research completed).

Other projects:

"Criteria for Water Resource Investment," U. S. Army Corps of Engineers (completed).

"Regional Effects of Public Investment," Economic Development Administration (in progress).

"Determinants of Spatial Form and Performance of the City," National Science Foundation (in progress).

"Impact of Space Activities on the National Economy," National Aeronautics and Space Administration (in progress).

"Unemployment among Central City Residents and the Transportation Network," U. S. Department of Housing and Urban Development (in progress). A number of conferences and seminars were held.

The postdoctoral program experience led to this evaluation: "It has appeared that the usefulness of the postdoctorate grant is materially increased by extending it for a period greater than one year."

The Institute publishes an irregular series of working papers on research findings. Number of publications by project include:

"Criteria for Water Resource Investment"	15
(May 1966-February 1968)	
"Design of Regional Accounts"	9
(June 1966-December 1967)	
(See Appendix H, item 16, for list of titles.)	
"Regional Effects of Public Investment"	11
(February 1967-July 1968)	
Miscellaneous	3

In co-operation with Communication Services Corporation, the Institute published *Reviews in Urban Economics* and *News in Urban Economics.*

University evaluation of CUE support

"We have made important progress toward creating the kinds of environment which truly can develop people who are both skilled and interested in working in urban and regional economics. The receipt of the CUE grant has materially assisted us in these efforts."

WAYNE STATE UNIVERSITY (economics)
Major faculty

Wilbur R. Thompson (full-time)
John M. Mattila (half-time)

Lon Polk (full-time)
Larry S. Singell (full-time to summer 1968)

Program highlights
First Year
Wayne State had a rather full complement of courses in urban and regional economics prior to the CUE matching grant. The start of CUE support found a large number of students well along in the field. A doctoral dissertation workshop was organized which all Fellows were required to attend, and each presented his work at least once.

The teaching staff in urban economics was greatly expanded.

The urban economics group will have a strong voice in the direction of development at a new Center for Urban Studies at Wayne State.

A year-long seminar on urban public policy was held for local decision makers.

Singell published four articles: two in *Quarterly Review of Economics and Business,* plus articles in *American Journal of Economics and Sociology* and *Urban Affairs Quarterly.* He also published two monographs and had three additional papers to be submitted for publication.

Second Year
Faculty members are engaged in a number of community activities, reflecting interest in public policy issues:

Thompson is board chairman, Southeastern Michigan Transportation Authority. Thompson is chairman of a forthcoming conference on urban goals and strategies. Polk is chief economist for the Detroit Metropolitan Area Transportation and Land Use Study.

The faculty will staff a new two-course sequence at the University of Michigan during the coming year while that university seeks to make a regular appointment in urban economics.

Three or four doctorates in urban economics are expected annually for the foreseeable future.

Faculty research topics include: general analysis of urban development; estimates of Detroit Gross Metropolitan Product; urban poverty problems.

University evaluation of CUE support
"The urban economics program was greatly accelerated by the CUE grant." Singell writes: "The CUE support has been instrumental in getting me established in the field of urban economics."

BROWN UNIVERSITY (economics)
Major faculty
       Benjamin Chinitz
Other faculty
       George Borts

Institutional organization
Departmental program in regional economic development established in 1957, under grant from Ford Foundation. Program extended to cover urban

economics on basis of CUE grant of $25,000 over a two-year period matched by an equal amount from Brown University.

Program highlights

Program provides for financial support for predoctoral and postdoctoral research fellowships.

Program also involves the organization of a research workshop. Focus is on the measurement and evaluation of economic activity in the urban environment.

Chinitz is writing a book entitled *A Primer in Urban Economics.*

University evaluation of CUE support

"Urban economics was encouraged by the CUE grant."

UNIVERSITY OF CHICAGO (economics)
Major faculty

George S. Tolley

Other faculty

Brian J. L. Berry
Charles Upton
John L. Gardner
Richard W. Parks
Peter Goheen

Institutional organization

The unified urban economics program involves the School of Business, Department of Economics, and the Center for Urban Studies, University of Chicago. Both economics and business administration offer urban economics as a field at the Ph.D. level.

The University of Chicago met all the CUE conditions except the availability of a full-time senior urban economist in the program. The commitment of half of George Tolley's time to the field, and the recruitment of three young urban economists to support the program, were the basis for a CUE grant of $45,000 to the university.

Program highlights

Tolley gave an advanced graduate course entitled *Economics for Urban Policy Decisions.* Some of Tolley's recent publications include "The Residence Site Choice" in *Review of Economics and Statistics,* and two book manuscripts in preparation: "Benefit-Cost Analysis in Regional Development" and "Open Area Economics."

An urban economics workshop held a series of meetings under the direction of Tolley and Parks.

New appointments of individuals committed to the urban field included:

Charles Upton, Assistant Professor, School of Business
John L. Gardner, Faculty Fellow (Urban Economist),
    Center for Urban Studies
Richard W. Parks, Assistant Professor, Economics
Peter Goheen, Assistant Professor, Geography

124

Faculty research topics: residential and commercial land values, local government expenditures, local development policy, relief and welfare programs.

University evaluation of CUE support:
"Our program is now being expanded under the research grant by CUE."

IOWA STATE UNIVERSITY (economics)
Major faculty
> Arnold M. Faden
> James R. Prescott

Other faculty
> Karl A. Fox

Institutional organization
Urban economics is a component of urban-regional economics analysis. The regional phase was started first, followed later by urban economics. Hence, early dissertations in the field had a regional economics emphasis.

Program highlights
Course offerings have substantially expanded in the last several years.

Faden conducted the graduate classes in Location Theory and Urban Economics. He is preparing a book entitled *"The Foundations of Spatial Economics,"* to be published by the Johns Hopkins Press. An article "Industrial Location in the Euclidean Plane" is to be published in *Geographical Analysis,* Vol. 1, No. 1.

Fox served on the Committee on Regional Accounts and has contributed numerous research papers dealing with functional economic areas, spatial equilibrium models and regional accounting. Some recent publications:

"Metamorphosis in America: A New Synthesis of Rural and Urban Society," chapter in *Changes in the Small Community,* Friendship Press.

The Role of Growth Centers in Regional Economic Development, report for the Office of Regional Economic Development.

James R. Prescott conducted seminars in urban-regional economics and state-local finance. Current research activities include: "Rental Formation in Federally Supported Public Housing," *Land Economics,* August 1967; "Experimental City: Comprehensive Planning for a Quality Urban Environment," UCLA Urban Seminar; "An Economic Simulation Model for Metropolitan Development Planning" (with Walter Mullendore); "An Econometric Model of Small Towns" (with William Lewis).

University evaluation of CUE support
"CUE grants have been essential to providing a balanced program in urban economics."

NEW YORK UNIVERSITY (public administration)
Major faculty
> Dick Netzer
> Ralph Kaminsky

Oscar Ornati (1967-68)
Thomas Stanback (1968-69)

Other faculty

Mark A. Haskell
Peter S. Albin
Bruno Stein

Institutional organization

The CUE grant is to the Graduate School of Public Administration and the Graduate School of Business Administration. Most of the graduate course work and research in the field is housed in the School of Public Administration. Urban economics is accepted as a field in economics as well as the schools cited.

Program highlights

The CUE grant has been used to support an interdepartmental workshop. The graduate schools of Public Administration and Business Administration conduct this workshop in the form of a joint seminar in urban economics. The purpose is two-fold: to stimulate student interest in urban economics and to offer students who had already taken courses in the field further opportunity for study.

The seminar is in its third year. It has enrolled roughly a dozen students in each year, and has been attended by additional students on occasion. Kaminsky has had primary responsibility for organization and administration of the seminar; typically, three or more additional faculty members participated in the sessions. The seminar has increasingly served as a testing ground for student and faculty research in urban economics (research outside the CUE program); it is the principal integrating mechanism for the various urban economics activities at New York University.

Faculty research topics: Local public finance and intrametropolitan location; public services and the future of the New York region's older cities; New York City finances; poverty and the Manhattan labor market; minority group lack of access to suburban housing and jobs.

Kaminsky is developing a text on urban economics.

Netzer and Kaminsky are concerned with urban problems in a development context for Colombia and San Salvador, respectively.

University evaluation of CUE support

"The CUE grant, for the Urban Economic workshop, has acted as a catalyst indicating external recognition and bringing economics and business administration into joint activities with Public Administration."

UNIVERSITY OF PITTSBURGH (economics)
Major faculty

Edgar M. Hoover
David F. Bramhall

Other faculty

Gordon C. Cameron (1967-68)
Gordon A. Marker (1967-68)

126

David Houston (1967-69)
Jack Ochs (1968-69)
Roger Riefler (1968-69)

Institutional organization

Research and teaching in urban economics is carried out at the Center for Regional Economic Studies.

Program

CUE support of $23,000 was allocated for the following:

1. A "partial-fellowship" fund of $10,000 supports graduate students in summer during the thesis-writing phase of their work. These students are employed as part-time assistants in the department, at university expense, during the two-term academic year. From CUE money they are given summer stipends and an allowance for research expenses to make it possible for them to devote one or more summers wholly to dissertation research and writing.
2. One three-year predoctoral fellowship in urban economics is awarded to a graduate student of exceptional promise. It is designed to support him during six terms of course work and dissertation writing in residence at the university. The total amount allocated for this fellowship is $13,000.

CUE support was also used in the establishment of a "distinguished external lectureship" for an initial three years. This is an arrangement with an urban economist at some other institution to make a prescheduled series of around half-a-dozen one- or two-day visits to Pittsburgh during a term, to present an integrated *course* of lectures and/or discussions, for which academic credit is given if deemed appropriate. The expectation is that a sequence of integrated lectures presented by one man in this fashion will lead to a publishable volume; and that if the lectureship works out well during the initial three-year period, it will be found worth continuing from internal or other external funds.

There is a 50-50 matching of costs between the university and CUE. In each of the three years, $2,500 is budgeted for the visitor's honorarium (out of which he is expected to pay his own travel expenses). The total cost of $7,500 is met by $3,750 from CUE and a like amount from university funds.

Center faculty engage in basic research in urban and metropolitan regional studies, and in applied research on the Pittsburgh metropolitan area.

Hoover recently served on the Advisory Group, Regional Economic Development Institute; Bramhall served as consultant, Ford Foundation Urban and Regional Advisory Program in Chile.

Appendix M

List of Participants in Programs of the Committee on Urban Economics, 1960-68

This appendix lists participants at CUE conferences (described in Appendix J) and recipients of CUE research grants (Appendix H) and communication grants (Appendix I). Staff members of RFF are not included. Each participant's institutional location is given as of the time of his participation.

Key to Abbreviations:
HR   = Conference on Urban Human Resources
RA   = Conference on Urban Regional Accounts
UPE = Conference on Urban Public Economics
UEC = Conference on Urban Economics
Grant = Recipient of urban economics research grant or communications grant.

The number after the abbreviation indicates conference number in a series; thus UPE 1 indicates the first Conference on Urban Public Economics. Form of participation is shown after the conference abbreviation; at HR 1, all participants were discussants.

Ackoff, Russell; University of Pennsylvania (UPE 1—Author)
Adamson, King; Wayne State University (Grant 1960)
Albin, Peter S.; New York University (Grant 1968)
Aronson, Robert L.; Cornell University (HR 1, HR 2—Discussant)
Artle, Roland; University of California, Berkeley (RA 1—Discussant)

Bailey, Martin J.; University of Chicago (Grant 1961)
Banfield, Edward A.; Joint Center for Urban Studies, MIT–Harvard (UPE 2 —Author)
Barnett, Harold; Washington University (RA 1—Discussant, RA 2—Chairman, UEC—Discussant)
Baumol, William J.; Princeton University (UPE 1—Author)
Becker, Gary S.; Columbia University (HR 1)
Beckman, Martin; Brown University (RA 1—Discussant)
Berman, Edward B.; The Mitre Corporation (RA 1—Author)
Bleile, George; Northwestern University (Grant 1961)
Bogue, Donald J.; University of Chicago (RA 4—Discussant, UEC—Discussant, Grant 1965)
Borts, George H.; Brown University (RA 1—Author, RA 2—Discussant, RA 3— Author, RA 4—Discussant)

128

Bramhall, David F.; National Planning Association (RA 4—Discussant)
Brazer, Harvey E.; University of Michigan (RA 2—Discussant, UPE 1—Discussant)
Buchanan, James; University of Virginia (UPE 1—Discussant, UPE 2—Author)
Bunting, R. L.; Cornell College (HR 2—Author)
Burkhead, Jesse; Syracuse University (RA 1—Discussant, RA 2—Author, UPE 2—Discussant, UEC—Author)

Campbell, Alan K.; Syracuse University (UEC—Author)
Capron, William; Brookings Institution (RA 3—Author)
Chinitz, Benjamin; Brown University (RA 1—Author, RA 4—Discussant, UPE 2—Author)
Cohen, Henry; City Government of New York (HR 1)
Colm, Gerhard; National Planning Association (RA 1—Discussant, Grant 1960, 1961)
Creamer, Daniel; National Industrial Conference Board (RA 1—Discussant)
Curran, Donald J.; Canisius College (Grant 1963)
Czamanski, Stanislaw; Cornell University (RA 4—Discussant)

Davis, Otto A.; Carnegie-Mellon University (UPE 2—Author)
Delwart, Louis; National Planning Association (RA 1—Author)
Douty, H. M.; Bureau of Labor Statistics (HR 2—Chairman)
Downs, Anthony; Real Estate Research Corporation (UPE 2—Discussant, UEC—Discussant)
Dyckman, John; University of California, Berkeley (RA 3—Discussant, UPE 1—Discussant)

Easterlin, Richard; University of Pennsylvania (HR 2—Discussant)
Eckstein, Otto; Harvard University (RA 3—Discussant, UPE 2—Discussant)
Eisenpreis, Alfred; Allied Stores Corporation (RA 3—Discussant)

Favor, Homer E.; Morgan State College (Grant 1962)
Ferguson, Charles E.; Duke University (RA 2—Discussant)
Fitch, Lyle C.; Institute of Public Administration (RA 2—Discussant, RA 4—Discussant, UPE 1—Chairman, UEC—Discussant)
Fleisher, Belton M.; University of Chicago (HR 2—Author)
Fox, Karl A.; Iowa State University (RA 2—Discussant, RA 3—Author, RA 4—Discussant)

Garrison, William L.; University of Illinois at Chicago Circle (RA 4—Discussant, UEC—Discussant)
Gilman, H. J.; Rutgers University (HR 2—Author)
Givens, Meredith; Institute of Public Administration (HR 1)
Goldner, William; University of California, Berkeley (HR 2—Author)
Greenwald, Douglas; McGraw-Hill Publishing Company (RA 1—Discussant, RA 3—Discussant)
Gross, Alvin; Pittsburgh Plate Glass Company (RA 3—Author)
Guthrie, Harold; University of Kentucky (HR 1, HR 2—Author, Grant 1961)

Hansen, Alvin H.; Harvard University (Emeritus) (UPE 1—Chairman, UEC—Chairman)

Hansen, W. Lee; University of Wisconsin (HR 1, HR 2—Discussant, RA 3—Discussant)

Harris, Britton; University of Pennsylvania (RA 1—Discussant, RA 2—Author, UEC—Author, Grant 1964)

Hayes, Frederick; Urban Renewal Administration (RA 3—Discussant)

Heller, Walter W.; University of Minnesota (UEC—Author)

Henderson, James M.; University of Minnesota (RA 1—Discussant, RA 2—Author)

Herman, Robert; State of New York, Budget Division (RA 3—Discussant)

Hirsch, Werner Z.; University of California, Los Angeles (RA 1—Author, RA 2—Discussant, RA 3—Author, RA 4—Author, UEC—Author, Grant 1964)

Hochwald, Werner; Washington University (RA 1—Discussant)

Hoffenberg, Martin; University of California, Los Angeles (RA 4—Discussant)

Holton, Richard; U. S. Department of Commerce (RA 3—Discussant)

Hoover, Edgar M.; University of Pittsburgh (RA 1—Author, RA 3—Chairman, RA 4—Discussant, UEC—Author)

Houston, David; University of Pittsburgh (RA 4—Discussant)

Huff, David; University of California, Los Angeles (Grant 1961)

James, Thomas; Stanford University (RA 3—Discussant)

Keyes, Scott; University of Illinois (Grant 1962 and 1966)

Kistin, Helen; Joint Center, Massachusetts Institute of Technology and Harvard University (Grant 1960)

Klarman, Herbert; Johns Hopkins University (HR 1)

Koffsky, Nathan M.; U. S. Department of Agriculture (RA 3—Discussant)

Korbel, John; University of Wisconsin (HR 2—Author)

Labovitz, I. M.; Library of Congress (UPE 1—Discussant)

Lamale, Mrs. Helen; Bureau of Labor Statistics (HR 1)

Lampard, Eric E.; University of Wisconsin (UEC—Author)

Lampman, Robert; University of Wisconsin (HR 1)

Lansing, J. B.; University of Michigan (HR 2—Discussant)

Legler, John B.; Washington University (RA 4—Chairman)

Leibenstein, Harvey; University of California, Berkeley (UPE 2—Author)

Leven, Charles L.; Washington University (RA 1—Author, RA 2—Author, RA 3—Chairman, RA 4—Author and Chairman, Grants 1966)

Lichfield, Nathaniel; University College, London (UPE 1—Author, UPE 2—Author, Grant 1962)

Lindblom, Charles; Yale University (UPE 1—Discussant)

Lowry, Ira S.; The RAND Corporation (RA 2—Discussant)

McKean, Roland N.; The RAND Corporation (UPE 1—Author, UPE 2—Discussant)

Mack, Ruth P.; Institute of Public Administration (HR 2—Chairman, RA 2—Discussant, RA 3—Discussant, UPE 1—Author, Grant 1962)

Manvel, Allen D.; U. S. Department of Commerce (UPE 1—Author)

Margolis, Julius; Stanford University (UPE 1—Author, UEC—Author, Grant 1965 and 1966)

Marshall, F. Ray; University of Texas (HR 1, HR 2—Author)

Martinson, John; Communication Service Corporation (Grant 1966)

Mattila, John M.; Wayne State University (Grant 1960)

Miernyk, William H.; University of West Virginia (RA 4—Chairman)

Milliman, Jerome W.; Indiana University (RA 3—Discussant, RA 4—Discussant, UPE 1—Discussant, UPE 2—Chairman)

Mincer, Jacob; Columbia University (HR 2—Discussant)

Moore, F. T.; Development and Resources Corporation (RA 1—Discussant)

Moses, Leon N.; Northwestern University (RA 1—Discussant, UPE 1—Discussant, Grant 1961)

Musgrave, Richard A.; Harvard University (UPE 1—Discussant, UPE 2—Discussant, UEC—Discussant)

Mushkin, Selma J.; Council of State Governments (HR 1, RA 3—Author, RA 4—Discussant, UPE 1—Author, UEC—Chairman, Grant 1967)

Muth, Richard F.; Washington University (HR 2—Discussant, RA 1—Discussant, UEC—Author)

Netzer, Dick; New York University (RA 2—Author, UPE 1—Discussant, UPE 2—Discussant, UEC—Author)

Niskanen, William; Office of Assistant Secretary of Defense (RA 2—Author)

Northrup, Herbert; University of Pennsylvania (HR 2—Discussant)

Ornati, Oscar; New York University (UEC—Author)

Orcutt, Guy H.; University of Wisconsin (RA 1—Author)

Pechman, Joseph; Yale University (UPE 1—Chairman)

Pendleton, William C.; The Ford Foundation (RA 4—Chairman)

Perlman, Mark; University of Pittsburgh (HR 1, HR 2—Author, Chairman)

Petersen, James W.; The RAND Corporation (RA 1—Discussant)

Pfister, Richard L.; Indiana University (HR 2—Author)

Price, Douglas; Syracuse University (UPE 2—Discussant)

Raymond, Richard; Brown University (Grant 1962)

Rees, Albert; University of Chicago (HR 2—Discussant)

Richards, John; Texas Western University of El Paso (HR 2—Author)

Ritter, Lawrence; New York University (HR 1)

Rivlin, Alice; Brookings Institution (UPE 1—Discussant)

Rothenberg, Jerome; MIT (UPE 1—Discussant, UPE 2—Author)

Ruggles, Nancy; Yale University (RA 1—Author, RA 4—Chairman)

Ruggles, Richard; Yale University (RA 1—Author, RA 4—Chairman, UEC—Author)

Sacks, Seymour; Syracuse University (UPE 1—Author)

Saffran, Bernard; University of California, Berkeley (UPE 2—Discussant)

Schaaf, A. H.; University of California, Berkeley (Grant 1961)

Schaller, Howard G.; Indiana University (UPE 1—Chairman, UEC—Discussant)
Schnore, Leo F.; University of Wisconsin (RA 2—Author)
Schwartz, Charles F.; International Monetary Fund (RA 1—Discussant)
Scitovsky, Tibor; University of California, Berkeley (UPE 1—Discussant)
Segal, Martin; Dartmouth College (HR 1, HR 2—Author, Chairman)
Shapiro, Perry; Washington University (RA 4—Chairman)
Shoup, Carl; Columbia University (UEC—Discussant)
Smith, Wallace F.; University of California, Berkeley (Grant 1965)
Sonenblum, Sidney; National Planning Association (RA 1—Author, RA 2—Discussant, RA 3—Discussant, RA 4—Author, UEC—Author, Grant 1960, 1961)
Stein, Jerome L.; Brown University (RA 1—Author)
Steiner, Peter; University of Wisconsin (UPE 2—Discussant)
Stolnitz, George J.; Indiana University (RA 2—Author, UEC—Author)
Striner, Herbert; Upjohn Foundation (RA 3—Discussant)
Strotz, Robert; Northwestern University (UPE 1—Discussant, UPE 2—Author)

Tabor, Stephen; University of Chicago (Grant 1965)
Terry, Edwin F.; Federal Reserve Bank of Kansas City (RA 2—Author)
Thompson, Wilbur R.; Wayne State University (RA 3—Author, UPE 1—Discussant, UEC—Author, Grant 1960 and 1964)
Tiebout, Charles M.; University of Washington (RA 1—Discussant, UPE 2—Author)
Tolley, George S.; North Carolina State University (UPE 2—Discussant)
Tullock, Gordon; University of Virginia (UPE 2—Author)

Vickrey, William; Columbia University (UPE 1—Author, UPE 2—Author)
Vogeley, William A.; U. S. Department of the Interior (RA 3—Discussant)

Ward, Benjamin; University of California, Berkeley (UPE 2—Author)
Weimer, Arthur M.; Indiana University (UEC—Chairman, Grant 1962)
Weisbrod, Burton; University of Wisconsin (HR 1, UPE 2—Author, Grant 1960)
Wheaton, William L. C.; University of Pennsylvania (Grant—1960)
Whinston, Andrew; Yale University (UPE 2—Discussant)
Wilson, James Q.; Harvard University (UPE 2—Author)
Winsborough, Halliman H.; Duke University (RA 2—Discussant, Grant 1963)
Wood, Robert; U. S. Department of Housing and Urban Development (UPE 1—Discussant, UPE 2—Chairman, UEC—Chairman)

RFF BOOKS RELEVANT TO URBAN ECONOMICS

The Quality of the Urban Environment: Essays on "New Resources" in an Urban Age. 1969. Harvey S. Perloff, ed. 344 pages. Paper, $6.50.

Issues in Urban Economics. Harvey S. Perloff and Lowdon Wingo, Jr., eds. 1968. 678 pages. Cloth, $15.00; paper, $5.00.

The Suburban Apartment Boom: Case Study of a Land Use Problem. Max Neutze. 1968. 182 pages. Paper, $5.00.

Revenue Sharing and the City. Walter W. Heller, Richard Ruggles, et al. 1968. 124 pages. Cloth, $6.00; paper, $2.50.

Converting Land from Rural to Urban Uses. A. Allan Schmid. 1968. 116 pages. Paper, $4.00.

Regional Accounts for Policy Decisions—papers presented at the Conference on Regional Accounts, 1964, sponsored by the Committee on Regional Accounts. Werner Z. Hirsch, ed. 1966. 244 pages. Cloth, $6.50.

Land Use Information: A Critical Survey of U. S. Statistics, Including Possibilities for Greater Uniformity. Marion Clawson with Charles L. Stewart. 1966. 420 pages. Paper, $6.00.

Environmental Quality in a Growing Economy—essays based on the RFF Forum lectures of 1966. Henry Jarrett, ed. 1966. Second printing 1968. 188 pages. Cloth, $5.00.

A Preface to Urban Economics. Wilbur R. Thompson. 1965. 428 pages. Cloth, $7.50; paper, $2.95.

The Public Economy of Urban Communities—papers presented at a 1964 conference sponsored by the Committee on Urban Economics. Julius Margolis, ed. 1965. 272 pages. Paper, $5.00.

Elements of Regional Accounts—papers presented at the Conference on Regional Accounts, 1962, sponsored by the Committee on Regional Accounts. Werner Z. Hirsch, ed. 1964. 240 pages. Cloth, $6.00.

Cities and Space: The Future Use of Urban Land. Lowdon Wingo, Jr., ed. 1963. 268 pages. Cloth, $6.50; paper, $2.45.

Public Expenditure Decisions in the Urban Community—papers presented at a 1962 conference sponsored by the Committee on Urban Economics. Howard G. Schaller, ed. 1963. 208 pages. Paper, $3.50.

Human Resources in the Urban Economy—papers presented at a 1962 conference sponsored by the Committee on Urban Economics. Mark Perlman, ed. 1963. 278 pages. Paper, $4.50.

Design of Regional Accounts—papers presented at the Conference on Regional Accounts, 1960. Werner Hochwald, ed. 1961. 302 pages. Cloth, $7.50.

Transportation and Urban Land. Lowdon Wingo, Jr. 1961. 144 pages. Paper, $2.50.

Books from Resources for the Future, Inc., may be ordered from bookstores or from The Johns Hopkins Press, Baltimore, Maryland 21218.

Designed by Sheila Ekers.
Composed in Optima text and Czarin display
by Port City Press, Inc.

Printed offset by Port City Press, Inc.
on 60-lb. Merion Offset.

Bound by Port City Press.